The
Subtropical
Garden

The Subtropical Garden

Photographs by Gil Hanly
Text by Jacqueline Walker

TIMBER PRESS
Portland, Oregon

'The universe is full of magical things patiently
waiting for our wits to grow sharper.'

Eden Philpots

First published 1992
Paperback edition published in North America in 1996 by

Timber Press, Inc.
The Haseltine Building
133 S.W. Second Avenue, Suite 450
Portland, Oregon 97204, USA
1-800-327-5680 (USA and Canada only)

Reprinted 1997, 1999, 2001, 2002

ISBN 0-88192-359-1

Cover design by Sarah Maxey
Cover photograph by Gil Hanly
Printed in Hong Kong through Colorcraft Ltd.

Contents

Preface

An alternative title for *The Subtropical Garden* could be *The Exotic Garden*, for the words 'exotic' and 'subtropical' are used here interchangeably and are concerned less with climate than with an approach or style. Rather than being guided by the conventions of cool-climate gardening, *The Subtropical Garden* suggests a refreshingly different way of creating a garden unfettered by tradition.

The purpose of this book is to spark ideas. It is not a plant reference book and may need to be used in conjuction with one—see the list of suggested reading at the back of the book.

The speculative aspect of growing some of these plants should also be emphasised. There may be readers who say of a certain plant, 'But it won't grow here', which could translate as 'I tried it and it died'. This book should encourage such people to try again. The more experimenting we do, the more we build up our knowledge of what will grow and what will not. Success will be aided by plant breeders who introduce fresh genetic material.

For such readers, and for those who have yet to try, *The Subtropical Garden* offers the incentive.

Acknowledgements

We'd especially like to thank all the people who spent time showing us their gardens and kindly allowed us to take photographs.

We are also grateful for the help and advice of: Graeme Arnott, David and George Austin, Rod Barnett, Robin Booth, Keith Boyer, Willy Coenradi, Gary Cooke, Peter Endicott, Dick Endt, Russell Fransham, Wendy Galbraith, Phil and Georgina Gardener, Geraldine Gillies, Max Goodey, John and Pauline Isaachsen, Andrew Lilburn, Bryan McDonald, Joan and Peter Money, Tony Palmer, Graeme Platt, Peter Raine, Brian Saunders, Noel Scotting, Ted Smythe, Lou Thackwray, Len Trotman, Sandra van Der Mast and John Whitehead.

Gil Hanly and Jacqueline Walker

Introduction

The subtropical garden is a garden of luxuriant foliage, where form takes precedence over flowers. It's a garden lush in undergrowth, spiked above with palm or tree fern fronds, punctuated by suspended epiphytes and vibrant flowers, with a backdrop of climbing vines and a foreground of blazing bromeliads. In its drier areas it flaunts swords in bold clumps, thick-fleshed aloes and swollen succulents. It's a dynamic, year-round garden, where warmth makes for rapid growth.

This is a garden to quicken the pulse.

Subtropical gardens are for warm climates, both moist and dry. The term subtropical is used here not in the strict geographical sense but in reference to climates where the summers are warm and winters are mild and frost-free. So even within a cool-climate garden, the term could apply to those parts that are sheltered and warm. In areas with high rainfall or moisture-retentive soil and shade overhead, lush-leaved aroids such as philodendrons, monsteras and alocasias thrive. In drier parts of the same garden, or in low-rainfall or coastal gardens, the appearance may be more of desert than jungle, with aloes, agaves and yuccas the dominant plants. In such gardens, moisture-loving plants can still be grown by creating ponds and bog areas. In moist soils the 'dry' plants can be raised up on rocks or logs, or positioned under dry eaves. With careful planning, it is possible to grow both moisture-loving alocasias and dry-ground aloes side by side.

The Subtropical Garden promotes imaginative planting without dictating rules of design or following established traditions. Gardeners will be inspired as much by an untamed forest as by any school of thought—though it's true that some influences come from Asia and the Pacific Islands, as well as

A *Furcraea* species, with its skirt of spent leaves, and *Agave americana* (foreground) make a strong impact in drier parts of the garden.

Opposite, above: Natural building materials such as timber and river stones are in keeping with the lush planting typical of subtropical gardens.

Opposite: The bright central colours in this cluster of bromeliads are echoed in the brilliant magenta flowers of the ground-cover *Heterocentron elegans*.

Previous page: This mixed waterside planting is dominated by lush, large-leaved aroids and a banana. The brilliant splashes of colour come from two vireya rhododendrons, as well as pink impatiens and a bergenia.

from arid Central American gardens and those of Brazil, where the landscapes of Roberto Burle Marx have made their distinctive mark.

The plants in the subtropical garden make statements, not suggestions. The emphasis is on architectural form and foliage. Flowers are often incidental, because colour comes from other sources—from ribs etched on leaves, foliage splashed with stripes or spots; from bromeliads cradling centres aglow with fire; from fronds, spathes and striking serrated edges. Where flowers do feature, they are in dazzling, festive colours—reds, oranges, yellows, bright pinks and purples. In gardens with a greater proportion of foliage plants, these high-voltage colours are absorbed and accentuated by the green density of foliage.

Subtropical gardens contrast with cool-climate gardens in a number of ways. Cool-climate gardens perform colourfully in spring but thereafter may lose impetus, whereas the subtropical garden, after a minimal but discernible flush of new growth in spring, goes on throughout summer and autumn getting better and better. Nor is autumn the end. All those months of growth that a mild climate favours pay dividends at the onset of winter, with the lushest and loveliest often coming last. The lull comes in late winter and early spring.

Another advantage is that impatient gardeners wanting fast results do not have to wait long. Warmth with humidity can produce astonishing growth rates—there's a joke among English settlers new to high-rainfall regions that the shrub that in England needs a trim after three years, in the subtropics calls for a chainsaw.

Subtropical gardens have few precedents or documented traditions to draw upon for inspiration. Just as today the funding and direction of scientific research is determined by consumer demand, so in the eighteenth and nineteenth centuries plant hunting was directed by those northern Europeans who had gardens and wealth. Interest in tropical and subtropical flora was limited to academic botanists and a handful of hothouse-owning gentry, while the big demand was for species that could grow outdoors in temperate climates. Plant hunters were instructed accordingly, and in Asia, where plants were picked over long before collectors ventured to Central and South America, high-altitude plants were sought. The result today is a vast body of knowledge about temperate plants, and a smaller but still-growing literature on the cultivation of tropical and subtropical plants and their use in garden design.

Many of the plants listed here come from those regions of Central and South America that might be described very generally as subtropical, while a lesser number come from Africa, northern Australia and Southeast Asia. Not a great deal is known about their cultivation outside their native areas, so everyone growing these plants is contributing to a body of knowledge that is far from complete. Information about the failure of some of the rarer species can be as useful as that about the success of others. Growing these plants is a speculative business. Sceptics may wish to sit back and wait until tried and proven plants flood the retail market, not wishing to gamble their money or their labour. Bolder gardeners, however, will see potential in every seedling and in every garden niche—and their confidence will often be rewarded.

For geographers, the term subtropical means those areas of the globe bordering on the tropics where the climate is warm and moist. Here a looser definition is assumed, including areas with warm to hot summers and mild, frost-free winters with temperatures falling to a possible 5°C, and rainfall ranging from 1000 to 2000 mm a year.

In areas that are not strictly subtropical, it is possible to create an artificial microclimate that closely approximates these conditions. To geographers and meteorologists, the term 'microclimate' describes the climate within 2 m (6.5 ft) of the ground over a very small area. This includes both hot and cold spots, adverse (for plants) or favourable. Over recent years, however, the word has been used in a broader, non-scientific sense to mean the warm and sheltered spots that occur naturally or, more often, that buildings and contemporary living places have created. Gardens protected by wind-breaks, screens and trellises; patios, entertaining areas (often half indoors and half outdoors), courtyards; open gardens where terracing has produced sheltered niches; recessed corners and protected pockets that face the sun—all of these are examples of artificial microclimates.

Microclimates can also result from the urban 'heat island' effect. A large city, which lights, heats and powers itself 365 days a year, will transmit heat to its surrounding inner suburbs. This is especially noticeable at night. Closely positioned buildings trap more heat than open spaces do, which is why country areas seem cooler at night while city gardens continue to receive and retain warmth from the centre.

This garden in full sun is sparsely planted with architectural specimens such as *Agave attenuata*, *Cycas revoluta* and a bed of *Sansevieria trifasciata* (foreground).

Opposite, above: *Aloe thraskii* is an imposing succulent for dry gardens.

Opposite: These three *Archontophoenix cunninghamiana* have a colourful underplanting including the red-leaved *Iresine lindenii* and the orange-flowered *Aloe arborescens* x *ferox*.

Any discussion of temperatures leads inevitably to a consideration of global warming and the greenhouse phenomenon. While the subject is too complex to be discussed in any depth here, some observations can still be made. It is important to keep in mind one of the basic rules of science: that all changes should be viewed in perspective. The monitoring of changes over a ten-year period, for example, must be set against other ten-year periods, as these changes could be minor fluctuations or cycles. When measured against aeons in the life of the planet, changes such as the current warming seem small, and professionals are understandably reluctant to assert that these are dangerous or irreversible. Fossil evidence shows that over millions of years there have been many such changes. The crucial point, however, is that the planet was not then home to 5000 million humans. If research is confined

13

to the last few centuries, when the human population gained momentum and the ability to observe such phenomena, evidence of global warming within this period is beyond dispute.

The first observation has to do with local soil temperatures. The soil temperature in any artificial microclimate is likely to be higher than that of the surrounding soil—more so when the soil has been newly obtained or newly created through organic decomposition—and this cannot be used as evidence of general soil warming. But soil in the open ground where crops are extensively cultivated is a different matter. A number of horticulturists who have been working their land over many years have recorded rises in soil temperature over sufficient land areas and during sufficiently long periods to provide evidence of soil warming. Their data may not satisfy scholars, but it should be enough to satisfy gardeners who need encouragement to grow the warm-climate plants they once thought they couldn't grow.

The second observation concerns the germination of seeds. Several exotic plant enthusiasts who had for years collected seed in the tropics only to find that it failed to germinate outside these regions are finding that seed of the same species, newly collected from the same places, will now sprout. What has changed? Again, there's no scientific control and the explanation could lie in the genetic material, but the change does coincide with other observations of environmental warming.

The third observation is about light, in particular ultraviolet light. Higher than normal doses of UV light resulting from thinning of the ozone layer affect plants. It appears that some species—for example, *Cordyline australis*, the New Zealand cabbage tree—are being triggered into blooming excessively, 'flowering themselves to death', and one explanation put forward is that this is due to an increase of UV light. Other species known to be sun-loving now seem to suffer in full sun but perform better in part shade. Large-leaved *Ficus* species and vireya rhododendrons are two examples. It could be that such plants are vulnerable to UV overdoses. A number of experienced gardeners advocate erring on the side of shade when siting plants.

Aside from exploiting microclimates—or creating them specially with walls and windbreaks—there's the matter of planting, feeding and caring for these plants. The subtropical garden is generally a low-maintenance garden. It is not as demanding as more formal, temperate gardens in terms of cultivation, seed sowing, pruning and preening, lifting and replanting. It doesn't call for fastidiously edged borders or parallel standards. It more closely resembles untamed nature.

This path is bordered with mature specimens of nikau, *Rhopalostylis sapida*, underplanted with clumps of the dark-leaved *Clivia miniata*, ferns and, in the foreground, colourful foliage plants, including calathea, stromanthe and several different kinds of bromeliad.

An attractive combination of contrasting textures—tree ferns, dark-stemmed colocasias and bright-flowered impatiens.

Mature tree ferns and nikaus, *Rhopalostylis sapida*, provide the shady environment preferred by impatiens, foliage begonias, clivias and these pale pink-flowered Japanese anemones.

Gardening in the subtropics requires a different approach from cool-climate gardening. This difference can be illustrated by a conversation that took place between two gardeners, one from a temperate and the other from a subtropical homeland. They were discussing the wear on their tools, the gardener from the cool, dry climate claiming he'd worn down his fork prongs to stubs. 'Good heavens', said the gardener from the warm climate, 'I never touch a fork, except occasionally when I'm turning compost. But I can wear out a pair of secateurs in six months!' The point is that gardeners in the subtropics rarely dig—they layer. They build up raised beds; they start off new plants in rings of bark or tree fern; they compost; they mulch; they shred up garden clippings and add these; they layer and then layer again. Their plants want warmth, and mounded materials are warmer than the soil beneath. And by layering, they reproduce as closely as possible the processes going on in forests, on mountainsides and in gullies around the subtropical latitudes of the globe. This is the way these plants grow in the wild; and this is how the subtropical garden will succeed. It was once believed that rainforests were growing on the richest soil on earth. This fallacy was washed away with the heavy rains in Brazil, when cleared patches of jungle proved to be as barren as the forest they once supported was lush. Fertility resided only in the top few inches and layers on the forest floor. Once the forest was cleared, deep digging yielded only leached clay. The moral is: don't dig down; build up.

The strong forms of these *Strelitzia* species are shown to advantage against a plain background.

One benefit of this approach is that weeds will be fewer, and when they appear they can be easily pulled out by hand. As for the secateurs wearing

out, as anyone who lives in a warm, high-rainfall climate knows, the loving care a gardener lavishes on a plant is often rewarded with the embrace of an octopus!

One way of raising plants above the surrounding ground is to use planter rings made from material through which roots can eventually penetrate, such as tree fern trunk. A hollow cross-section, about 15–40 cm (6–16 in.) in diameter and 30–40 cm (12–16 in.) deep, is set in the ground to about one-third of its depth. The ring—with the plant in—is then filled (but not rammed tight) with a good mix of compost, fine bark and topsoil or peat moss that will allow the roots ease of growth and good drainage. Slow-release fertilisers can be added to ensure a good start. The poorer the quality of the soil or drainage below, the greater the need to raise up the growing medium, perhaps barely embedding the ring. Lest this be seen as likely to dry out quickly, remember that, when mulching, the mulch should be piled up outside as well as inside the ring (but avoid packing it against the plant's stem, as this will cause stem rot). Mulching retards moisture loss. Do this and four needs of your tender exotic will have been met: warmth, aeration, drainage and nutrition. In terms of watering needs, plants in planter rings come halfway between plants in pots and plants in the ground. They should be treated like pot plants at first and watered frequently, then, as their roots penetrate a wider feeding area, they can be watered less frequently.

The matter of watering deserves further consideration. The dictum to grow only those plants that will survive without water in addition to natural rainfall does make sense. To observe it means choosing plants carefully and being environmentally responsible. But exceptions should be allowed. One exception would be in the event of extreme drought (in which case bath water should be used before drinking water) and a second exception would apply to new plantings, which need help to get through the first few years. It might be argued here that in the wild young plants manage on their own. On the contrary, they don't. Nature compensates for losses with generosity. Of the dozens, hundreds, or perhaps thousands of seedlings from parent plants, only the toughest survive—a tiny percentage. The home gardener, with only one or two young plants of the species, aims for a 100 per cent success rate, and this involves doing everything possible to aid their survival. The third exception is the watering of containerised plants and, to a lesser extent, plants in rings.

Many tropical and subtropical plants are surface rooting, perhaps encouraged by high rainfall. To avoid damaging these roots, it's preferable to pull weeds out by hand rather than hoeing the ground. The surface roots take up nutrients during times of regular rain; during dry spells the plant relies on deep taproots to get moisture. Applying layers of compost and mulch will encourage the development of surface roots and thereby aid the nutrition of the plant.

Most subtropical plants are prolific feeders, particularly during the warmest months when they are actively growing, and will need feeding in addition to compost and mulch. Fertilisers should be applied before the main growth period. Gardeners who feel comfortable about using chemical fertilisers are advised to use preparations including nitrogen (N), phosphate

(P), potash (K), plus trace elements sulphur, magnesium and iron. These fertilisers are available commercially in slow-release and fast-release forms. Slow-release preparations give an even amount of nutrient over a given time (three, six or twelve months), while fast-release is available to the plant in ten days but has an active life of only six weeks. The NPK formula varies with different brands, but the following are suitable for general gardening: fast-release N12 P5 K14 or N6 P5 K6; slow-release N16 P3 K10 or N15 P4 K10. Containerised plants have the greatest need of slow-release fertilisers, since they have no access to anything else.

Gardeners who prefer non-chemical fertilisers find that foliage spraying improves growth. Diluted solutions of seaweed, fish manure and commercial preparations can be applied—as long as rain or watering is frequent. Foliar feeding should be avoided where leaves are dry for long periods. Neither water nor liquid feed should be applied to hot leaves in full sun.

Opposite: The distinctive leaf shape of *Sabal minor*, the dwarf palmetto palm.

Opposite, below: Brugmansias, with their beautiful white or coloured, hanging trumpet flowers, are essential in the subtropical garden.

The lushness and contrasting forms and textures of this planting give the garden a cool, restful atmosphere.

Fresh manure should be added to soils with caution; it is best when well rotted in compost. Sheep manure is sold as pellets; poultry manure can be used for plants preferring alkaline to acid soils; pig manure, if obtainable, is particularly good; a mixture of rotted horse manure and decomposed pine needles enriches acid soils.

Healthy plants are better equipped to resist pests and diseases, but in warm climates these can be a problem. Although they can be combated by chemical or organic means employed by gardeners everywhere, prevention is still of greater value than cure. Many experienced gardeners in warm climates believe that the following preventive practices are of more importance than any number of cures: close monitoring of plant health; good garden hygiene; planting schemes that mix species rather than segregate them; encouraging birds in the garden; companion planting; and the promotion of healthy plants from the very start. One supervisor of a large botanic garden reported that after years of spraying according to a systematic programme, whether pests were evident or not, he switched to spraying only in response to a problem, and this was confined to the individual branch or part of the plant under attack. He observed no increase in pests, and, in fact, after several seasons of the new regime, noticed an increase in bird life.

The design of the subtropical garden tends to be less formal than cool-climate gardens. It's likely to resemble the original wild habitat of its occupants more than the borders and hedges of temperate gardens, whose plants have been so long in cultivation that their origins may be lost.

The principles of good garden design apply in the subtropical garden as much as in any other garden. Before starting, get to know your site, decide what you need and what you want, and when you're sure of the look or style you are aiming for, work towards that end and don't be tempted by distractions. Make sure all the components contribute to the effect. Natural elements are usually more appropriate than artificial ones in the subtropical garden. A fallen log lying beside a shaded path and hosting a dozen fresh ferns can contribute more than an ornate balustrade or wrought-iron furniture. Classical statuary that fits so well in European gardens isn't always suitable for an exotic-foliaged garden. Asian or Pacific Islands ornaments may seem more fitting, especially where materials are of natural plant origin, such as bamboo screens, hollowed gourds, pottery urns, wood carvings or tree fern trunks.

Apart from their beauty as plants in the subtropical garden, tree ferns have a number of uses. The trunks can be used to make fences, walls or plant supports, the dark brown, fibrous texture making a fitting backdrop for climbing plants and flowering creepers, as well as for bromeliads and

The design of this garden is defined by the structural plants such as palms, bamboos and cycads. Low-growing ferns, grasses and other foliage plants soften the edges of the pond. Waterlilies will provide colour when in flower.

21

Simple wooden furniture is appropriate in subtropical gardens. The colour here is provided by the red-foliaged *Iresine lindenii*, or bloodleaf, which contrasts pleasingly with white impatiens.

The unusual *Begonia luxurians*, palm leaf begonia, from Chile, is grown as much for its palmate leaves as for its flowers.

epiphytes. Positioned crosswise on the ground, lengths of trunk can create paths, perhaps covered with wire mesh, which soon becomes invisible, for better foothold. If the felling of these forest natives seems alarmingly destructive, it is consoling to learn that, in New Zealand at least, tree fern species are harvested from non-indigenous pine plantations that are commercially cleared, not from native forests. But the practice's real redemption is that the cutting down of a tree fern is not the end of its life. New ferns sprout away from the cut trunks— provided they're kept moist—so that a cut log can produce a dozen or more infant ferns. These progeny can be left in place to grow or planted out in suitable sites in the garden. Tree fern bark is not coarse and makes a good mulch; it's useful for covering paths and, of course, it's an ideal compost ingredient.

Don't forget the use of rocks. Smooth, small rocks closely positioned imitate stream beds; great chunks of rock piled high resemble mountain slopes and are wonderful for aloes and other succulents, cycads, bromeliads and plants that will grow in a minimum of soil. Such large rocks supporting plants of such dramatic shape are the exotic garden's version of the low-profile pebble gardens for alpine plants in cool climates.

There can still be a place for formality and hard landscaping in the subtropical garden. For example, few city gardens have space for a natural, bog-edged water garden, and hard-edged pools that have to fit into tight areas tend to look formal. But alongside these, massive- leaved jungle plants such as *Cecropia peltata* and *Anthocleista grandiflora* can transform the scene into something exotically lush and dramatic. By concentrating on these feature plants—

and there really are some exciting species to discover—a planting scheme that is restrained in diversity but boldly conceived, using sculpture plants with real impact, can be stunning.

The key elements of the subtropical garden are: a lush density of plants, which means areas of deep shade; the use of natural materials; an emphasis on foliage rather than flower, on shape rather than colour; the use of brilliant and intense colours rather than subdued tones, where colour does occur; and, above all, drama in the plants themselves.

Those gardeners in the enviable position of starting with a blank canvas can begin by defining the framework of the garden—the plant architecture—selecting structural plants with strong vertical and horizontal lines, bold and

This mixed waterside planting includes the strong forms of tree ferns, bamboo and the large-leaved *Gunnera manicata*.

dramatic foliage, and flowers in hot, tropical colours. Then come the smaller plants, the climbers and ground-covers, accents and fillers, which complete the picture.

This book can help with inspiration and ideas. While plant descriptions are brief and basic, they give some indication of size and site preference and will motivate readers to search further. For more detailed plant information, consult the reference works in the suggested reading list on page 169.

Mention of a subtropical garden almost always brings to mind subtropical fruit: avocados, feijoas, guavas, passionfruit, babacos and a host of other delicious edibles, many of which have only recently been introduced into home gardens. Single specimens of such fruit can be easily accommodated in small areas and can complement an exotic-foliage garden. A detailed study of subtropical fruit is beyond the scope of this book, but the following species are worth trying: casimiroa, or white sapote, *Casimiroa edulis*; cherimoya, *Annona cherimola*; pawpaw and babaco, *Carica* species (see also page 51); lucuma, *Lucuma obovata*; pepino, *Solanum muricatum*; naranjilla, *Solanum quitoense*; Cape gooseberry, *Physalis peruviana*; tamarillo, *Cyphomandra betacea*; casana, *Cyphomandra casana*; avocado, *Persea americana*; feijoa, *Acca sellowiana*; jaboticaba, *Myrciaria cauliflora*; tropical guava, *Psidium guajava*; capuli cherry, *Prunus capollin*; sweet granadilla, *Passiflora ligularis*; and *Ziziyphus jujuba*.

No book on subtropical gardens can ignore the work of Roberto Burle Marx. Recognised by the American Institute of Architecture as the 'creator of the modern garden', and acclaimed for his inspired designs, his vision, his spectacular landscapes and his profound knowledge of tropical American flora, Burle Marx, more than anyone else, has marked the gardens of the twentieth century.

Burle Marx's thoughts and ideas are so often quoted that his account of his youthful awakening is probably familiar. But because it explains so well the extent to which gardens, plants and, in fact, everything about the landscapes we create around us is culturally moulded, it's worth retelling.

Roberto Burle Marx grew up in Rio de Janeiro, in a house where the garden was well stocked with vegetables and the flower gardens conventionally grown in colonial settlements: roses, carnations, dahlias and gladioli. At the age of eighteen, Burle Marx accompanied his German-born father to Berlin to study music, drama and painting. There he visited the Berlin-Dahlem heated botanic gardens, which housed collections of Brazilian flora. The experience awed and challenged him. It was a catalyst. Thereafter, his one aim was to return to Brazil and grow the plants he'd never before known or appreciated.

Rethinking and re-seeing our gardens is what this is all about: the ability to visualise a setting for exotic and subtropical plants that may well grow more successfully and more easily than plants we've previously grown. The plants are available; 'new' plants are continually reaching the market; cultural information is accessible; the tools, the soils, the shelters and the hard materials are at hand. The vision and the commitment are up to the gardener.

The banana is synonymous with tropical and subtropical gardens. *Musa* x *paradisiaca* is the fruiting species most commonly grown, and there are also several ornamental species with striking foliage and colourful bracts and fruit.

Plant
Architecture

Plants with strong visual impact make up the framework of the subtropical garden. Rather than relying on artifical structures, the plants themselves define the garden's architecture. Here are palms, bamboos, trees and tree ferns, as well as bold sculptural plants such as bananas, yuccas, aloes and cycads—plants that command attention.

There are architectural plants for every garden, be it large or small: dwarf palms or towering specimens; slow-growing trees or rapid-growing tree ferns; neglect-proof grasses; plants that can take wind, salt air, full sun or deep shade. And many of these designer plants with spectacular shapes come from semi-arid regions, so they will adapt perfectly to dry parts of the garden.

While form takes precedence over flowers among architectural plants, colour is not absent. As well as myriad shades of green, there's foliage in red, bronze, pink, orange, olive, rust and deep burgundy—the flamboyant pink of one *Cordyline terminalis* cultivar is dazzling. As for flowers, they're not down at ground level but can be seen festooning branches of trees such as tabebuias, cassias and coral trees in brilliant, tropical colours.

Architecture of this kind calls for planning and imagination. But the task can be made easier by growing young specimens in containers, which can be moved around until the plants are ready to be placed out in their permanent positions. Experimenting is half the fun! Tall vertical lines can be used as backdrops; species with large leaves will provide useful shade; the eye-catching coronets of cycads may be foreground features, while the tough, easy-care sword plants such as astelias, sansevierias and yuccas can adapt to almost any situation.

27

Palms

The plant that epitomises the exotic garden is surely the palm. These strongly vertical plants are the flagstaffs of the tropics, bringing to mind images of rainforests, islands, oceans and oases. Few other trees are so instantly recognisable—their silhouette is unmistakable.

Though equally effective as permanent garden features or contained in pots on patios, palms look best planted in groups—especially as mixed species, or if each plant is at a different stage of maturity. This approach imitates their natural growth patterns in the wild, where no two would be the same size: fresh and fern-like when young, ribbed pleats unfolding exuberantly in mid-youth, then spiking the sky at head height, and finally fanning the breeze overhead when fully mature. When well grown, even palms in containers will make a small suburban garden look lush and exotic.

Palms may be single-trunked specimens or naturally clumping. Of those species listed here, six are clumping, and these will obviously take up more space than those with single trunks. It's not true that palms are only suitable for large gardens. Nor is it true that all palms are interminably slow growing. There are many slender-trunked, quite miniature palms, just as there are many speedy growers. As for growing requirements, there are three: moisture, good-quality soil, and shade when young. This goes for any species you choose to grow, though at maturity some tolerate full sun and drought while others are better in semi-shade with moisture.

Palms have other advantages. They make landscape planning easy because their dimensions and shape can be accurately predicted—unlike shrubs, for example, whose projected dimensions are usually far from precise. While the crown foliage may cast welcome shade, the tall-growing species have no lower branches to interfere with plantings at the base, so sun-loving species can be planted to encircle the palm, where branching trees could prohibit such cultivation. They also make splendid lawn specimens, as turf can be grown right up to the trunk, which will not be damaged by close mowing.

Palms also have tidy root systems, which don't wander off and choke drains the way horizontally rooting trees often do. The root balls are densely fibrous, hard and compact, allowing palms to grow for years in containers before needing more room—and allowing them to be transplanted, fully grown, to new sites, bumping up the profits of many a land developer. Should extra soil be mounded up against the trunk of a palm, it has the ability to produce adventitious roots at the base. A retaining wall and garden around

Previous page: This section of a large subtropical garden features structural plants with strong, architectural forms. The clumping *Phoenix reclinata* (centre) is flanked by bamboo and a *P. canariensis*. Planted among the rocks are several handsome specimens of *Cycas revoluta*.

Right: Bold fronds of *Phoenix canariensis* and *P. reclinata* against the sky repeat the shape of *Cycas revoluta* (foreground) while contrasting with the horizontal lines of the pool and loggia. The feathery palm in the centre is a young *P. roebelinii*.

28

A pair of potted *Trachycarpus fortunei* channel the eye to a more distant group of *Syagrus romanzoffianum*, a fast-growing, adaptable palm with notably feathery fronds.

the base of most trees would be harmful to their trunks, but with palms this helps rather than harms their growth, for they react by rooting rather than rotting. However, soil should be piled up in moderation—not more than 30–40 cm (12–16 in.) at a time.

Another advantage of palms, particularly for people with little spare time, is that they require minimal maintenance apart from the removal or gathering up of dead fronds; they don't need pruning, and they're largely insect-free.

Give palms a good start with what one experienced grower calls a $5 hole for a $1 plant. Dig it as deep as possible, break up the surrounding soil, and, if it's dry, fill the hole with water first—which is also a good way of testing the drainage. If the ground is clay and the drainage is poor, scoop out only a very shallow hole and mound the soil up using a tree fern ring (see page 18). Use plenty of compost and a sprinkling of slow-release fertiliser. The width of the hole should be twice that of the pot the plant has been growing in. With these preparations completed, take your well-watered palm (preferably having immersed it, still in its container, in water for an hour beforehand) and place it in the hole, firm the soil around the roots, and add a layer of mulch.

Many palms like light, sandy soils, though these may need more organic supplements than heavier ones. Although most species prefer slightly acid soils, some grow well in alkaline conditions. These include: *Brahea armata*, *Butia capitata*, *Chamaerops humilis*, *Phoenix canariensis*, *Phoenix dactylifera*, and *Sabal* and *Washingtonia* species.

As for moisture requirements, by far the majority of palms come from habitats where the air humidity is high and the soil is moist, or where there are underground watercourses available to them—desert palms are rarities compared with the rest of the world's species, and even they must have access to underground water. Similarly, by far the majority must have shade when young—in their natural habitats, young plants grow up under the shade of parent palms. Water young palms well and keep the sun away from them. If the air is dry, water from overhead. And, as with all garden irrigation, confine hot-season watering to the cool hours of evening or early morning. It goes without saying, of course, that mulching aids moisture retention.

Given favourable conditions, young palms can grow quite fast—some as much as 2.5 m (8 ft) in five years, though most take a bit longer. If there is no hurry, or a landscaping scheme is planned that will develop over many years, try raising palms from seed. It's very much cheaper, and seed is often available free from collectors and palm society members. Although clumping palms can be propagated by detaching new shoots, every palm reproduces naturally by seed. Raising your own in this way can be very satisfying. While

Left: *Phoenix reclinata* has a tendency to sucker. This plant has had some of its suckers removed to reveal the slender, ringed trunks.

Right: The *Chamaedorea* genus contains well over 100 species; while leaf form varies, they share in common the thin, elegant trunks evident in this *Chamaedorea* hybrid.

31

This waterside planting of *Phoenix roebelinii*, the dwarf date palm, shows very young palms with fresh, feathery fronds.

Opposite, above: *Sabal minor* is a fast-growing palm native to the subtropics and well suited to small gardens.

Opposite: This group of stately windmill palms, *Trachycarpus fortunei*, have had their dead fronds cut away, giving them a uniformly groomed appearance. Note the dense fibre covering the trunks.

seed from many flowering trees and shrubs—to say nothing of powder-fine petunia seed—can be fiddly to handle, seeds from palms are large, smooth and fleshy, and some are surprisingly heavy. In fact, the largest seed in the plant kingdom, weighing up to 20 kg (44 lb), comes from the Seychelles Islands' native coconut palm, *Lodoicea maldivica*. Palm seeds need warm temperatures (22–30°C) to germinate. Any seed-sowing mix will do, provided it includes peat to retain moisture. Cover them with a layer about as thick as their own depth, keep them moist and wait for them to germinate. On average, this takes from three to twelve months, though it also depends on the freshness of the seed. *Washingtonia* seed has been recorded as sprouting in only ten days, while other species have sat for eighteen months or so before shooting up a perfectly healthy sprout.

The following descriptions are of palms—from the smallest up—which grow easily and well in a subtropical climate.

Among the smallest palms are a handful of *Chamaedorea* species, which make splendid garden specimens. *C. ernesti-augusti* is a slow-growing, small (1 m/3 ft) shade-lover—an understorey palm in tropical rainforests. It has a single, slender stem, with rings caused by leaf scars, deeply notched leaves and, when in flower, unusually conspicuous (for a palm) bright scarlet flowers. This species is not common in cultivation. *C. elegans*, or the parlour palm, is sold by the thousand as an indoor plant. It, too, has a single, slender stem, but its dark green leaves are pinnate. It requires warmth and shelter, and outside in the subtropics it needs the boost of a warm microclimate to succeed. *C. concolor*, another with a thin stem and shiny, pinnate leaves, grows to around 1.5 m (5 ft) tall. Like *C. elegans*, it is sensitive to cold. *C. costaricana* is a strong-growing (to 2.5 m/8 ft), clumping palm but is cold-tolerant. It can survive even cool temperate climates if given shelter. It will also stand exposure to sun when mature; and as a tub plant, it is decorative both indoors and out.

Chamaedorea metallica is altogether different. As the name implies, the deep blue-green leaves have a metallic sheen, which is enhanced when they are wet, making it a very desirable palm. The leaf is rather heart-shaped and is held horizontally atop the slender stem. *C. metallica* is a miniature (to almost 1 m/3 ft) and it, too, needs plenty of shade and moisture. *C. radicalis* is another small, shade-loving palm but without a stem. It has arching, pinnate leaves and is easily grown. Of all the *Chamaedorea* species that will grow in the subtropical garden, *C. microspadix* is by far the easiest—see below. All species need plenty of water, especially when young, and plenty of shade; too much exposure to sun tends to make the leaves yellow and vulnerable to thrips and spider mite.

Sabal minor, the dwarf palmetto palm, bears stiff, fan-shaped leaves from a very short trunk, though it is sometimes described as trunkless. Native to the southern states of the United States, it is tolerant of poorer and shallower soils than most palms, likes air movement and sun, and doesn't

mind cold—all of which make it a good garden palm. It grows to 2 m (6.5 ft) and bears small, fragrant flowers when quite young.

Phoenix roebelenii is another small species. Often called the miniature or dwarf date palm, it has a slender trunk and feathery, arching fronds, and grows to about 2.5 m (8 ft). It is cold-tolerant, responds well to feeding and mulching, and will grow in full sun or part-shade.

Rhapis excelsa, as widely grown indoors as *Chamaedorea elegans*, has the common names of lady palm and bamboo palm. The latter name is apt, since this 2 m (6.5 ft) tall palm grows in clumps, with its deep green, fan-shaped leaves borne on stems from ground level right up, making a dense, bamboo-like barrier. Easily grown in containers and in the garden, this palm looks its best in partial sun with regular watering. *R. humilis* is very similar in every respect but is a little more open at the base.

Lytocaryum weddellianum (syn. *Cocos weddelliana*) is a little-known palm from Brazil and is not easily obtained. It is also fairly slow growing, reaching about 2 m (6.5 ft). However, it is particularly graceful, with a slender trunk and shining leaves, and grows in both low and bright light.

Chamaedorea microspadix is a clumping, bamboo-like palm similar in habit to *Rhapis excelsa*. It has many virtues: it is fast growing under good conditions, tolerates a wide range of temperatures, germinates readily from seed, and is easily divided and transplanted. This wonderful, small (around 2.5 m/8 ft) palm also produces decorative orange-red fruits. *C. seifrizii*, the reed palm, recognised by its stiff, erect, clumping habit and its mid-green, glossy fronds, divided into narrow or broad, spaced leaflets, grows to 3 m (10 ft) in height. *C. tepejilote* has a single, slender stem, which produces dark, pinnate fronds from loose crowns at around 4 m (13 ft) or more in height.

An interesting, small to medium-sized palm, native to Australia, is *Linospadix monostachya*, with the common name of walking-stick palm. Its exceptionally slender stem is never more than 3 cm (1.5 in.) thick, but because of its sturdiness and the small knob at its base, just below ground level, it makes an excellent walking-stick. During the First World War it provided thousands of walking-sticks for returning wounded soldiers. The fronds are divided into irregular, dark green leaflets. In summer mature plants produce bright orange fruits. To grow this 3–4 m (10–13 ft) palm successfully, give it complete shade and organically rich, mulched, well-drained soil. It withstands cool climates but is very slow growing—it is often regarded as a collector's item.

Somewhat bigger, but still within the range of small palms for small

This lush grove is evidence of how close together palms can be planted. Here the central palm *Rhopalostylis baueri* var. *baueri* is flanked on either side by *Archontophoenix cunninghamiana* (showing hanging inflorescences), while in the foreground to the right is a young *Phoenix canariensis*. The large-leaved plant in the centre is *Strelitzia nicolai*.

gardens, are *Chamaerops humilis*, the European fan palm, and *Livistona chinensis*, the Chinese fan palm. A clumping palm, *C. humilis* comes from Mediterranean regions and is as tough as nails. Provided it has sound drainage, it can take just about anything, including poor soils, wind and frost (which is not to say that young plants don't respond to good care). This widely grown fan palm has a mature height of about 4 m (13 ft). *L. chinensis*—native to Japan and parts of Taiwan and China—is also very tolerant and easy to grow. It is a single-trunked, fan-leaved palm, up to 5 m (16.5 ft) tall, and is characterised by fronds with drooping end segments.

Butia capitata, though often misleadingly called *Cocos capitata*, is not the coconut palm—the true coconut is *C. nucifera*. *B. capitata*, the jelly palm, is a stout-trunked palm of pleasing shape. The fronds have blue to blue-green, feather-like leaves and are strongly arched, long and recurved. It likes full sun, is cold-tolerant and grows slowly to 5 m (16.5 ft). The edible fruits are used for making jams and jellies, hence its common name. *B. yatay*, another jelly palm, also has edible fruits. It's a slow-growing species with bluish fronds, like *B. capitata*, but it is taller and will eventually reach 13 m (43 ft) or more.

Trithrinax acanthocoma, from Brazil, is a little-known palm that grows well in both the tropics and the cooler subtropics. It has two very favourable attributes and one distinctly unfavourable: the pleated fan leaves are large, neat and handsome, while the edible fruits are delicious. However, the trunk's base has long, treacherous spines extending horizontally from a covering of brown fibre, which probably evolved centuries ago to deter predators from taking the fruits. This species should therefore be handled with the utmost care. *T. acanthocoma* grows to about 2.5 m (8 ft) and will flower and fruit when young. Though not at present available commercially in any quantity, it will be sold more readily in future, and it's certainly a palm to watch out for.

Neodypsis decaryi, the rare and exotic Madagascar palm, has a distinctive 'three-sided' trunk that is short in relation to its very long and arching fronds. It must have full sun and good drainage, and can be a bit fussy in some locations, but it is sufficiently unknown to make it a collector's item.

Two palms that grow to around 5, 6, or at most 7 m (up to 23 ft) tall are: *Hedyscepe canterburyana*, from higher altitudes on Lord Howe Island, which thrives in temperate to cool subtropical conditions, with plenty of moisture and as much wind as comes its way; and *Howea forsteriana*, the famous kentia palm from Lord Howe Island. Market demand for this popular indoor plant is so strong that seed collecting by Lord Howe Islanders has become an important local industry. The straight and very slender trunk is conspicuously ringed, and the leaf fronds form a graceful crown. But what keeps *H. forsteriana* so much in demand is its valuable tolerance of extreme conditions: sun or shade, hot or cold, dry or humid air, coastal salt winds, even low light. As well as being indoor plants, kentias are excellent garden palms, especially when planted in groups. Though slow growing to 7 m (23 ft), they are good for beginners.

Opposite: *Butia capitata* is one of the easiest palms to grow, tolerating both cool temperatures and full sun, as well as a wide range of soils. The photograph on the far left shows the emerging spathes covering the inflorescence. The fruit of this species are edible.

Opposite, below: The silvery sheen at the base of this young *Hedyscepe canterburyana* distinguishes the species. It's a handsome, medium-sized palm, wind-tolerant but requiring moisture.

Howea forsteriana, previously the kentia palm, has fine, spine-tipped fronds and well-ringed, straight trunks. It grows well as an indoor plant when young and can be planted outside to reach maturity. A yucca dominates the foreground.

A group of young *Washingtonia robusta* palms makes a pleasing focal point in this mixed garden. Washingtonias are adaptable to a wide range of conditions including cool temperate regions. The foreground is dominated by large-leaved aroids; the orange-flowered plant on the right is *Hedychium greenii*, scarlet ginger.

Pritchardia gaudichaudii comes from the Hawaiian island of Molokai, where it grows in cliff-hanging colonies. It is useful for planting in coastal areas with humidity and fast drainage. *P. gaudichaudii* has particularly handsome, 1 m (3 ft) wide, pleated fans and grows to around 7 m (23 ft). In cooler subtropics, though, it is unlikely to reach this height, and it is best suited to a hotter climate.

One of the most decorative of clumping palms is the golden cane palm, *Chrysalidocarpus lutescens*. The light yellowy green fronds are slightly twisted or arching, giving the clump a full, fluffy appearance. It is cold-sensitive when young, tolerating sun at maturity, which is at around 7 or 8 m (23–26 ft). It is a wonderful tub or container plant but needs shelter from extreme conditions.

Brahea armata, the Mexican blue hesper palm, grows with a single trunk to 8 m (26 ft) and has several notable attributes: it is drought-tolerant once

established (it comes from rocky gullies of Arizona); it has fan-shaped leaves in an attractive blue-grey colour; and its cream flowers, which are held on long, arching stems, are very ornamental.

Rhopalostylis sapida, New Zealand's native nikau palm, bears its fronds in erect clusters, rather like a giant feather duster. It needs moisture and rich soil to do well, growing 6–8 m (20–26 ft) from shade to sunlight. The larger Norfolk and Kermadec Islands palms, *R. baueri* var. *baueri* and *R. baueri* var. *cheesemanii* respectively, with fronds more arching, lax and graceful, and with a decidedly faster growth rate, are more desirable for the garden.

Trachycarpus fortunei, the Chinese windmill or chusan palm, grows 6–8 m (20–26 ft) or taller and is also cold-tolerant. It is known to grow better in Tasmania and Dunedin than in the equatorial tropics, and will grow even in England. It likes full sun but is otherwise fairly undemanding and fast growing.

Caryota ochlandra, the Chinese fishtail palm, is the most cold-tolerant of

The fronds of young nikau, *Rhopalostylis sapida*, are handsome alongside the ringed trunks of mature specimens. This mixed underplanting is edged with the neglect-proof *Chlorophytum comosum* 'Vittatum'.

39

this genus, noted for its fishtail leaflets. Most are fully tropical, but *C. ochlandra* will tolerate even a touch of frost. It has a single trunk, a large crown, and the fishtail-like leaves have a slightly bluish tinge. It's a sought-after palm and grows to around 8 m (26 ft), but it is short-lived (about 20–25 years).

Of the many *Phoenix* species, the date palms, the only true fruiting date is the North African *Phoenix dactylifera*. *P. rupicola* is a medium-sized species that reaches 8 m (26 ft). It is a good choice for the home garden because of its narrow, soft appearance, unlike other stiff-fronded Phoenix palms. *P. canariensis*, the well-known Canary Island date palm, is much larger, to 18 m (60 ft), with a widespread crown of stiffly arching fronds. Its thick trunk has a rough pattern left by shed fronds. *P. sylvestris* is much less common, with blue-green to blue-grey fronds. *P. reclinata*, the Senegal date palm, grows to about 9 m (30 ft), but unless the suckers are removed it will form an impenetrable thicket.

Jubaea chilensis, from Chile, is extremely cold-tolerant (even young plants can take frosts) and extremely thick-trunked. Although not common and very slow growing, it's a magnificent 20 m (66 ft) palm—if it's obtainable.

Brahea edulis, the Guadalupe palm, reaches 10–12 m (33–40 ft). A useful palm, which has proved very adaptable to a wide range of temperatures, even tolerating cold and full sun exposure, *B. edulis* is grown in many countries for its fruit. These are small, round and black, containing seed pulp that is fleshy and sweet, and are produced in large numbers.

Another species with edible fruits, and one that belongs so much to cooler temperate regions that the subtropics may be too hot, is the South American Quito palm, *Parajubaea cocoides*. Growing to around 8 m (26 ft) in height, *P. cocoides* likes a fast-draining soil, bright light, sunshine and cool nights during summer.

There are a number of species of really tall palms, which grow to 15, 20 and even 25 metres (82 ft). Although gardeners restricted to balconies and patios can justifiably ignore them, they should not be dismissed for more spacious gardens. Maturity to that height can take many years—a lifetime in fact—so perhaps it's better to consider the life expectation of the gardener rather than that of the palm.

Washingtonia robusta, the cotton palm or California fan palm, is very easy to grow. The palmate leaves are bright green and the stems are covered in tan-coloured fibre. The old leaves hang down as a skirt but can be removed. *W. robusta* is fast growing, cold-hardy and will succeed in any reasonable soil but will grow more rapidly if watered. *W. filifera* has grey-green leaves fringed with white fibres. It is better suited to dry climates and tends to be spotted in areas of high humidity.

Archontophoenix alexandrae, the very popular, smooth-trunked king palm,

Three *Archontophoenix cunninghamiana* tower over the spiky rosette forms of *Aloe arborescens* x *ferox*, *Cycas revoluta* (the Japanese sago palm) and bromeliads. The palms show both new and ageing inflorescences.

The feathery fronds of young *Archontophoenix cunninghamiana* and the fine-leaved bamboo contrast with the bold foliage of *Ensete ventricosum*, the Abyssinian banana.

up to 20 m (66 ft) tall, with feathery, arching fronds, is widely grown throughout Australia, being native to the coast of Queensland. It is tolerant of salt air as well as cooler temperatures but must be protected from direct sunlight when young. It can be fast growing in good situations and responds well to feeding. *A. cunninghamiana*, the bangalow palm, is fairly fast growing, similarly handsome but grows even taller. This rainforest palm prefers shelter, and is readily damaged and can look scruffy if grown in the wind. *Archontophoenix* species are often referred to as seaforthia palms.

The queen palm, *Syagrus romanzoffiana* (syn. *Arecastrum romanzoffianum*), is a fast-growing (to 18 m/60 ft), sun-tolerant native of South America, worth growing for its slender trunk and arching, dark green fronds. It responds well to fertiliser and prefers an open site.

Euterpe edulis, the assai palm or jucara palm, is a slender-trunked species whose arching fronds bear thin, drooping leaflets. Indoors it's tolerant of dark conditions, but it grows best outside in rich, well-drained soil away from direct sunlight. Eventually this solitary palm from Brazil will reach 8–10 m (26–33 ft).

Rarely available, and even more intolerant of the merest chink of sunlight, *Ceroxylon quindiuense* is still worth seeking out— it's another tall species that takes a long time getting there.

Architectural Form and Foliage

Plants with graphically striking foliage are important architectural elements in the subtropical garden. There's nothing understated here—nothing dainty or delicate, filigreed or finicky—but bold sails of green sheeting, jagged wands, glistening paddles held horizontally at shoulder height, piercing swords and thick, leathery straps. With each of them, it's the shape that stops you in your tracks. Flowering is secondary to foliage. With such dramatic presence, their value to the gardener is that only a few are needed to achieve an instant effect.

All of the plants listed here are large (though not necessarily occupying large ground area). There's nothing much under 1 m (3 ft), and several reach an ultimate height of 10 m (33 ft) or more—though this could take a long time—so restricting their size by growing them in containers is also an option.

Consider first the *Musa* genus, the banana. For sheer surface area it has few competitors. It would be hard to devise a more dramatic shape than the arching fronds of the Abyssinian banana, *Ensete ventricosum*, except perhaps the airborne wheel of paddles of the travellers' palm, *Ravenala madagascariensis*. The best ornamental species for a cooler-than-tropical climate, the Abyssinian banana's wide and wonderful leaves, up to 6 m (20 ft) long and more in ideal conditions, with an attractive reddish midrib, will stay fresh and unblemished in a sheltered setting, unlike other more damage-prone relations. The Abyssinian's fruit are meagre, and hard unless cooked. *M. acuminata*, the dwarf banana, is smaller and shorter, up to 3 m (10 ft), and its leathery leaves have a satiny sheen. Its fruit are edible and fragrant.

The fruiting species grown commercially and in home gardens is *Musa* x *paradisiaca*. Don't ever say that these are large and messy plants that take up a lot of space or litter the lawn just for a bunch or two of something you can buy at any store on any day of the year. Instead, try eating a perfectly ripe, home-grown one—you'll be impressed. Once you've tasted the real thing and resolved to grow your own, prepare the best soil you can in a well-protected site with all-day sun, obtain a variety suited to your conditions, plant it deeply, water it well, especially in dry periods, and then wait for it to fruit, which it will do in a couple of seasons. Each plant dies after fruiting but leaves offspring in its place. As the clump grows, chop the central stems of dead plants into sections and pack them around the perimeter of the clump to form a raised edge. Apply layers of mulch within the contained area and use all the discarded debris from the plant to add to these layers, never allowing the base to be bare. As for the best varieties, since bananas are tropical, only those cultivars that have proved themselves in subtropical climates are worth trying. These include the 'lady finger'

Right, above: Impressive in both leaf and flower, *Musa velutina* is particularly suitable for smaller gardens, creating a tropical atmosphere wherever it grows.

Right: *Strelitzia nicolai* has large, paddle-like leaves and intriguing white flowers with dark purple-blue bracts—a dramatic combination.

varieties, the cultivar 'Mon Maree', and a Samoan variety called 'Misilu ki'.

Most of the other species need fully tropical conditions to perform well. When given a really warm microclimate, the black banana, *Ensete maurelii*, will thrive. Its rich, dark colouring is impressive. The red Assam banana, *Musa mannii*, is a dwarf species, up to 1 m (3 ft), and has olive-green leaves with red midribs. The dwarf ornamental species *M. velutina* is one of the smallest species (to 1.8 m/6 ft). An elegant plant particularly suitable for smaller gardens, it has showy, pink-red flowers and fruit. The flowering banana, *M. ornata*, has leaves to 2 m (6.5 ft) long and orange-yellow flowers with pink bracts.

Two less-common species that tolerate slight chills are *M. basjoo*, the Japanese fibre banana, which has bright green, shiny leaves up to 3 m (10 ft) long, and *M. sumatrana*, the leaves of which are blotched with red. The red-flowering banana, *M. coccinea*, is tender and fully tropical, and is grown as much for its fiery flower as for its foliage. It has oval, dark green leaves up to 1 m (3 ft) long, and in summer it bears yellow flowers enclosed in striking red bracts. These three species grow to a height of about 3 m (10 ft).

All bananas are gross feeders and need abundant moisture. The fruiting stems should be removed once flowering and fruiting are finished.

Strelitzia reginae, the bird of paradise flower, also a member of the *Musaceae* family and native of South Africa, grows effortlessly to 1.5 m (5 ft), with leathery, bluish green leaves and stiff stems from which emerge the bright orange flowers and dark blue bracts that look like crested birds' heads. *S. juncifolia* (syn. *S. reginae* var. *juncea*), the small-leaved bird of paradise or rush strelitzia, has needle-pointed leaves so thin as to be reed-like, forming a dramatic clump of the same size and with flowers similar to those of *S. reginae*. *S. nicolai* is a much larger species that can reach 6 m (20 ft) tall. The banana-like leaves are very imposing, and the flowers are white with a purple-blue bract. Strelitzias benefit from feeding and good watering, and respond especially well to grooming.

Ravenala madagascariensis, the travellers' palm, is one of nature's master-pieces. It's not strictly a palm—the common name refers to the value to travellers of the rain-collecting receptacles formed where the stem bases join the trunk. The precise fan formation, made up of leaves 3–4 m (10–13 ft) long, have made *R. madagascariensis* admired the world over. In the tropics it can reach 10 m (33 ft). It should be planted where it has the best wind shelter possible. Give it deep, rich soil, good drainage and plenty of moisture. The higher the windscreen, the better the leaf conditions, since once the uppermost sails extend higher than the shelter, the wind may soon ravage them.

The strong, architectural forms of these plants have a dramatic impact. The two palms at left are *Phoenix roebelinii* and *P. canariensis*; the low-growing palm by the water's edge is a young *P. roebelinii*; and the spiky, thin-trunked plant is *Cordyline stricta*.

A large, spreading shrub that flaunts its crinkly, lobed leaves horizontally is *Tetrapanax papyriferus*, the rice-paper plant. The leaves are rough, puckered and deeply incised, and when young, the leaf surface is covered with a white felt, which changes with maturity to a darker green and then to a rust colour. Mature leaves grow up to 35 cm (14 in.) across. The rice-paper plant is easy to grow and, given plenty of water, will rapidly reach 4 m (13 ft), to provide a dramatic subject on its own or shade for under-plantings. It has the added virtue of being adaptable to sand, soil and salt winds. In summer it produces huge masses of cream-coloured flowers, followed by black berries in autumn and winter. *T. papyriferus* is indeed the source of rice paper, which is made from the pith of its stem and branches. There's also a less-common variegated form, *T. papyriferus* 'Variegatus', with attractive splashes of dark and light green and ivory.

Trevesia palmata, the snowflake plant, is an even larger-leaved cousin of the rice-paper plant. Its leaves are glossy, palmately lobed and often covered with tiny silvery dots—hence the common name. Or does the great leaf with its strong veins and jagged edges resemble a snowflake? Either way, it's an immensely impressive shrub or small tree, similar in growth habit to tetrapanax but with shinier and larger leaves that can measure more than 40 cm (16 in.) across.

Both *Tetrapanax* and *Trevesia* are members of the *Araliaceae* family. Other members of this group of plants include the familiar *Fatsia japonica*. This is a very accommodating plant found the world over; like many in the sub-tropical garden, it first became popular as a house plant before moving out-doors, though, unlike most of the others, it tolerates considerable cold. It grows to about 3 m (10 ft) and has deeply lobed, glossy, green leaves. Terminal clusters of green-turning-white flowers are produced in autumn. It grows and looks best in the shade.

Other *Araliaceae* include the familiar Queensland umbrella tree, *Schefflera actinophylla* (syn. *Brassaia actinophylla*). Its smooth and somewhat willowy branches bear symmetrical palmate leaves, which are a shiny, leathery green and very decorative. Although mature trees can reach 30 m (100 ft) in their native tropics (Queensland, New Guinea and Java), in the subtropics they are not as tall—though at any age and any height they are striking. *S. octophylla* is a native of Hong Kong, very similar in appearance but with slightly more upright leaves. *S. arboricola*, the miniature umbrella plant, is a dwarf species and very popular as an indoor plant. Outside, it makes an ideal, compact specimen for the small garden.

A number of species and hybrids in the *Araliaceae* family are native to New Zealand. These include the lancewoods—small trees bearing those thin, leathery, strap-like leaves with serrated edges typical of *Pseudopanax crassifolius*—as well as species with distinctive palmate leaves, such as *P. arboreus*, or five finger. *P.* 'Adiantifolius' is a hybrid with wide, lobed leaves (like large maidenhair fern leaflets); *P. discolor*, cold-hardy and easy to grow, is a five-finger shrub with bronze foliage; *P. laetus*, preferring a warm site, has much larger, palmate leaves, giving it a more tropical appearance (the richer the soil, the larger the leaves); and *P. lessonii* 'Gold Splash' is a cultivar whose name describes it exactly. All of these species benefit from good soil and plenty of moisture. When young, they need a semi-shaded site that allows them to grow up into the sun, although the lower-growing species are naturally understorey plants tolerant of quite heavy shade.

Another *Araliaceae*, not always obtainable but unmistakably exotic, is the evergreen *Oreopanax salvinii*, from Mexico. Its huge, lobed leaves are strikingly indented. Although it is grown as an indoor plant in the United States, it does well in the subtropics in a sheltered site with plenty of moisture.

Perhaps the most handsome member of the family, certainly tropical in leaf, is the New Zealand puka, *Meryta sinclairii*. Although occurring only rarely in the wild—its natural distribution was limited to several islands—it has taken easily to garden cultivation, where its dark green leaves, large and glossy, are admired all year round. Now beloved by landscapers, *M. sinclairii* will grow to a medium-sized, spreading tree and will enhance any spot with sufficient shade and moisture to get it started towards the light. Keep the roots shaded and let the upper leaves sparkle in the sun.

Another large-leaved species is the lustrous fiddle-leaf fig, *Ficus lyrata*. As a juvenile container specimen, it can be an arresting sight, with its large (38 x 20 cm/15 x 8 in.), vaguely violin-shaped leaves glistening in the sun. Give it moisture and feed it, and keep its roots shaded—it makes a neat patio plant. *Ficus elastica*, the India rubber tree, can also be kept as a container plant. The dark green leaves of the cultivar 'Decora' are considered outstanding. Both grow well as trees in the garden but need plenty of room. *F. religiosa*,

Opposite: *Schefflera actinophylla*, the Queensland umbrella tree.

Opposite, below: The glossy-leaved *Meryta denhamii* is a valuable small tree, like its relative the puka, *M. sinclairii*.

A dense backdrop of greenery, including ferns, palms and the foliage plants *Griselinia lucida* (right) and a *Pseudopanax* species, provides a foil to the brightly coloured, low-growing impatiens.

the sacred fig tree, and *F. benghalensis*, the banyan, are also useful landscaping plants when grown in containers. Giants in their native habitats, they can be kept as small trees in pots in the garden, where they can serve the useful function of plugging gaps or screening neighbouring eyesores. There are other *Ficus* species, however, that are naturally small. *F. auriculata* (syn. *F. roxburghii*), the ornamental fig, is wide-spreading but under 6 m (20 ft) in height. Its rounded, papery, slightly glossy leaves, up to 40 cm (16 in.) long, are its main attraction, though rivalled perhaps by the inedible globose fruits borne on the stems. *F. rubriginosa* 'Variegata' exhibits highly ornamental leaves marbled with cream and green; *F. triangularis* is another small ficus, bearing masses of small, greenish beige berries on woody branches. *F. benjamina*, the weeping fig, may grow to more than 10 m (33 ft) in favourable conditions but can be kept at almost any size. A beautiful evergreen tree, more common as an indoor plant, its weeping habit, slender branches and lustrous, deep green leaves produce a very elegant effect—highly recommended.

Dense and polished evergreen foliage can provide an effective backdrop for colourful low-growing or container plants. Dependable foliage trees of this sort include *Griselinia littoralis*, or kapuka, a fast-growing New Zealand native. However, this is probably outclassed by *G. lucida*, slower growing but with much larger, thick, glistening green leaves, which have made it very popular with landscapers. Though tolerant of most conditions, both griselinias grow best in semi-shade, up to about 8 m (26 ft), and are useful for coastal plantings.

Above: The large, glossy leaves and compact form of the New Zealand native *Meryta sinclairii* make it an ideal tree for small gardens.

Right: Foliage alone makes this subtropical garden lush and restful. Structural and textural interest come from the commanding Brazilian fern tree, *Schizolobium parahybum*, two species of *Schefflera* (foreground) and tall palms, as well as low ferns and other shade-loving plants.

The corrugated leaves of the New Guinea native *Dammaropsis kingiana* are so large and striking that it makes a splendid feature plant.

Right, top: The forest fever tree, *Anthocleista grandiflora*, has a head of spectacularly large leaves. It makes a marvellous specimen plant in a container or in the garden.

Right, above: Pawpaws, *Carica* species, have large, attractive leaves and produce edible fruit. Small enough for town gardens, they are fast growing and upright, with a satiny trunk patterned by leaf scars.

Pisonia umbellifera, the parapara, has similarly striking leaves—up to 30 cm (12 in) long—and a dense growth habit to about 4 m (13 ft). A variegated form, *P. umbellifera* 'Variegata', with dramatic splashes of cream, is much admired. It is commonly called the bird-catcher tree, because in late summer its fruits become very sticky and will trap small birds feeding on them until they die. Pisonias are at their best in semi-shade with plenty of moisture. They also make splendid container plants.

Anthocleista grandiflora is the exotic forest fever tree from South Africa. The leaves are paddles, over 2 m (6.5 ft) long and 50 cm (20 in.) wide, and its silhouette is palm-like, the bare trunk crowned with a head of these huge leaves. As a landscape feature it has tremendous impact, while its bare trunk allows for planting at its base (single-species mass plantings are particularly effective). Forest fever trees ultimately reach 6–9 metres (20–30 ft).

Cecropia peltata is another massive-leaved tree. Palmately lobed, the reddish leaves develop silver undersides as they age, a glistening sight when stirred by the wind. It's a robust, spreading tree with hollow stems and milky juice.

If *Cecropia peltata* has any competition for leaf size or drama, it would have to come from its relation *Dammaropsis kingiana*, whose leaves are quite astounding—as long as 60 cm (24 in.) and almost as wide, leathery, and deeply corrugated. It is native to New Guinea, where it grows to around 4 m (13 ft) tall, the trunk and relatively small branches overshadowed by its imposing leaves. It needs warmth and moisture.

Among the glossiest leaves of any tree are those of the New Zealand native karaka, *Corynocarpus laevigatus*—dark green, seldom blemished and densely produced. However, it's not just the high-lustre leaves that are eye-catching—in summer and autumn the fleshy berries turn golden and then bright orange. Young trees need shade and moisture, but at maturity (8–12 m/26–40 ft) they are undemanding.

One particularly stunning tree for the subtropical garden is *Schizolobium parahybum*, the Brazilian fern tree. This fast-growing (to 10 m/33 ft or more), deciduous native of Brazil puts forth its canopy of 1 m (3 ft) long, feathery leaves in spring, arching gracefully from the slender trunk—elegant and refreshingly different. *S. parahybum* needs sun and deep, rich, well-drained soil, slightly on the dry side.

Synadenium grantii, the African milkbush, is also grown for its giant leaves, which are slightly wavy at the margins, light green and traced with dark veins. It's a semi-succulent, evergreen shrub, which enjoys warmth and full sun, and grows up to 3 m (10 ft). There's also a less-common, red-leaved form, *S. grantii* 'Rubra'. *Ricinus communis* belongs in the same family (*Euphorbiaceae*). Popularly known as the castor-oil plant, its bright green, deeply lobed leaves are its main attraction. It is easy to grow well, and the erect, buoyant leaves are always fresh. It does, however, seed prolifically and can be hard to eradicate.

Carica papaya, the fruiting papaya, has a single slender trunk, which is patterned by the scars of shed leaves like a palm trunk. From the top sprout large and very ornate leaves, making it a neat and compact feature plant for a small garden. It is, however, a tropical species and may be difficult to grow in cooler climates. The mountain pawpaw, *C. pubescens* (formerly *C. candamarcensis*), is a hardier species commonly grown in the subtropics. It's a small tree with attractive foliage and bears bunches of pear-shaped, yellow fruit containing small black seeds. The babaco, *C. pentagona*, is also an attractive, straight-trunked tree but with superior fruit. Hanging in clusters round the trunk, the largest fruit at the bottom are equivalent in volume to a small football; the fruit higher in the cluster are smaller. Both skin and flesh are eaten, with no seeds to bother about. The delicious, juicy flesh is eaten raw but can also be cooked and is excellent in drinks.

Eriobotrya japonica, the loquat, is a small, evergreen tree with large leaves that make it much at home in the exotic garden. Its juicy, yellow-orange

An attractive tree with shiny, quilted leaves, the loquat, *Eriobotrya japonica*, bears delicious fruit.

51

fruit are delicious fresh or cooked, and it is easily grown in almost any soil, including clay.

Among the many structural plants that can make an important contribution to the exotic garden are members of the *Agavaceae* family. Some are drought-tolerant succulents, while others, such as dracaenas, need moisture; but all have distinctive silhouettes of erectly held, strap-like foliage tapering to sharp points. They include dracaenas, cordylines, yuccas and sansevierias.

Dracaenas are ideal architectural plants for small gardens. They are evergreen trees and shrubs, with striking foliage and distinctive form. *Dracaena marginata*, which has rich green leaves and red margins, produces a number of thin trunks of pleasing irregularity on which the tufts of foliage are held high. This species and *D. arborea*, which has wavy leaves with prominent midribs, both grow to small trees but can be kept as low-growing specimens in pots. *D. hookerana*, the leather dracaena, is a slow-growing species that has shiny leaves with translucent margins. *D. sanderana*, the ribbon plant, is a neat plant with slightly twisted leaves, pale green with cream margins. *D. fragrans*, which tends to have wider, more lax leaves, grows to around 2.5 m (8 ft). There are a number of variegated cultivars, such as 'Lindenii', with greenish yellow banding, 'Massangeana', with yellow-striped centres to the leaves, and 'Victoria', with silver streaking. *D. deremensis* reaches 2 m (6.5 ft) or more, with glossy, green leaves that arch as they mature. It, too, has produced several striking cultivars with variegated foliage. All dracaenas grow best in partial to full shade, with plenty of water and humus-rich soil. They can be heavily pruned if necessary.

Left: Dramatic form and foliage and the minimal use of vibrant colours characterise the subtropical garden. The pink-striped *Cordyline terminalis* (centre) is alongside a pawpaw, *Carica* species (right).

Above: Dracaenas are popular plants with striking foliage, and many new hybrids, such as this *Dracaena fragrans* 'Santa Rosa', have been raised.

Then there's the squat and solid single trunk of the dragon tree, *D. draco*, with its spiky eruption atop—not to everyone's liking but an undeniably dramatic species. Drought-tolerant, *D. draco* develops a spiky head of green or grey-green, lance-shaped leaves, and is slow growing to an ultimate height of about 5 m (16.5 ft).

Cordyline species are sometimes called grass palms because from a distance they look like palms sprouting clumps of coarse grass. The two best-known cordylines are undoubtedly *C. australis*, the New Zealand native cabbage tree, which is grown throughout the world, even in cool climates, and the rich-hued, tropical *C. terminalis*, or ti. Along with *C. australis*, and its strikingly variegated cultivar 'Albertii', other species native to New Zealand are *C. banksii*, which has flax-like, drooping foliage and especially white flowers; its bronze cultivar 'Purpurea'; the mountain cabbage tree, *C. indivisa*, a cold-tolerant, single-trunked species reaching about 8 m (26 ft) tall, with broad leaves; *C. kaspar*, endemic to the Three Kings Islands and a multi-branched species; and *C. pumilio*, the dwarf species, which has very thin, brown leaves and grows to less than 1 m (3 ft) tall. The more tropical *C. terminalis* has much broader leaves in pinks, reds and purples—decorator plants grown indoors in containers but able to make a splash outside. All cordylines have honey-sweet flowers.

Then there are the wonderful yuccas, drought-tolerant sentinels of higher altitudes and distant deserts, outstanding as garden features. They need space to grow and to be seen to advantage. The best-known species is probably *Yucca filamentosa*, often called Adam's needle, with a large rosette of sword-shaped leaves from which emerges, in summer, a stiff stem covered in

Left: From a commanding poolside position, these spear-like yuccas are undeniably dramatic.

Right: The spiky dragon tree, *Dracaena draco*, has been positioned in this corner setting for maximum effect. The low-key underplanting among the rocks accentuates the dramatic form.

54

pendulous, cup-shaped, white blooms. Both the plain and the variegated form, with its attractive cream margins, have extremely sharp points to their leaves—a good reason for giving them ample space away from pathways—and they also share the distinctive curly threads that hang from their leaf margins. *Y. aloifolia*, the Spanish bayonet, is a slow-growing shrub or tree, reaching about 4 m (13 ft). It has sword-shaped leaves with sharp points, and there are some colourful variegated forms, such as 'Quadricolor' and 'Tricolor'. *Y. carnerosana*, the Spanish dagger, will form a small tree with a thick trunk. It has stiff leaves to 80 cm (32 in.) long and produces a dense cluster of fragrant, white flowers. *Y. recurvifolia* reaches 2 m (6.5 ft), with a short trunk, and has recurved, dark, glaucous leaves. *Y. elephantipes*, the spineless yucca, is popular as a garden subject, as it grows and flowers particularly well in containers. Its toothed, dark green leaves are up to 1.2 m (4 ft) long, and it produces large clusters of bell-like, creamy white flowers in summer. Possibly the best choice for an urban garden is the trunk-less shrub *Y. whipplei*, which forms a compact head, less than 1 m (3 ft) high, of pointed, blue-green leaves. Its fragrant, white flowers are carried on a long stalk in early summer. All yuccas need sun. Their ability to grow in gravel and arid conditions makes them ideal plants for low-maintenance gardens. Note, though, that many of them are monocarpic—they die after flowering. However, they always leave behind infant plants at their base, and these will quickly grow to take their parent's place.

The genus *Sansevieria* is best known for the species *S. trifasciata*, the infamous, indestructible and inelegantly named mother-in-law's tongue. It

The vertical spears of *Sansevieria trifasciata* contrast with the clean, horizontal lines of this landscaping.

includes a number of striking species and cultivars to offer vertical interest in the garden. *S. trifasciata* grows to 1 m (3 ft), with stiff, upright spears patterned in green and yellow. *S. trifasciata* 'Laurentii' has bright creamy yellow leaf-margins to contrast with the deep green. There are also shorter cultivars, such as 'Hahnii' and 'Golden Hahnii' (to 35 cm/14 in.), with much wider leaves in rosettes. Sansevierias are worth considering, if only because they're so utterly easy to grow. And given a bit of moisture and nutrition, they'll produce fragrant flowers too.

Australia's ancient grass tree, *Xanthorrhoea australis*, has fine, green leaves up to 1 m (3 ft) long. The local name of 'black boy' refers to the trunk rather than the 'head'. Xanthorrhoea grow for hundreds of years.

Straight spears are also found in this rather military parade. *Dasylirion wheeleri*, the desert spoon, and *D. longissimum*, the Mexican grass tree, grow into rigid, bristle-like, grassy clumps, as does *D. serratifolium*. *D. glaucophyllum* is exceptionally dramatic, best described as a dense sphere of spiny rapiers. The spiny-margined leaves of *D. acrotriche* are brush-tipped. All these grass-like relations of cordylines and yuccas need sunny sites in fast-draining soil.

Tall, clumping reeds and grasses can also provide structural interest. The common South American pampas grass, *Cortaderia selloana*, can reach a height of 5 m (16.5 ft) or more in a clump almost as wide, and bears its silvery cream, silky plumes in summer. *C. jubata* has attractive pinkish plumes. Pampas grass can be relied on to grow in quite dry areas. More slender and lower growing is the toetoe, *C. richardii*, native to the South Island of New Zealand, while the North Island native, *C. splendens*, is comparable in size to the Argentinian species.

If pampas grass is not always welcome in the garden because of its razor-sharp leaf edges and habit of seeding prolifically, then bamboo (see page 66) or sugar cane, *Saccharum officinarum*, can fulfil a similar role. The latter grows rapidly into a clump about 3 m (10 ft) tall, and the canes mature at about nine or ten months. Also useful are the *Arundo* reeds, such as *Arundo donax* 'Versicolor', the bamboo lookalike with green-and-white variegated leaves (2.5 m/8 ft).

The wide leaf blades of the palmgrass, *Setaria palmifolia*, have a marvellously exotic appearance. These 50 cm (20 in.) long and 6 cm (2.5 in.) wide blades look more like juvenile (unseparated) palm leaves or the leaves of giant bamboo—to which it is related—than most grasses. *S. palmifolia* forms a clump about 1 m (3 ft) tall, and produces small, green flower-spikes in summer. Like all grasses, it grows best in moist, fertile soil, in semi-shade to full sun.

Flaxes (*Phormium* species) generally have wider leaves than grasses. They are easy to grow but respond well to generous watering. And they make splendid container plants. *Phormium tenax*, New Zealand flax or harakeke, has leaves 1–3 m (3–10 ft) long, usually more rigid than the smaller, less-common species *P. cookianum*. It will grow in a wide range of situations, succeeding equally well beside water or on a dry, windswept hillside. *P. cookianum*, the mountain flax or whariki, has leaves up to 1.5 m (5 ft) and is ideal for smaller gardens. Both species have attractive flowers, borne on tall, stiff stems, those of *P. tenax* being a dull red and those of *P. cookianum*

Top: The wide, corrugated leaves of palmgrass, *Setaria palmifolia*, form elegant clumps and add to the exotic appearance of the subtropical garden.

Above: *Astelia nervosa*, with its attractive, arching, silvery leaves, forms a compact clump and is an undemanding plant.

a yellowish green. A range of striking cultivars has been produced, including *P. cookianum* 'Tricolor', which has leaves striped red, yellow and green, and *P.* 'Dazzler', with leaves striped in bronze, red and pink. This cultivar produces red flowers in summer and grows to 2.5 m (8 ft).

Astelias, especially *Astelia nervosa*, are smaller cousins and very easy to grow. On the whole, they make tidier clumps than flax. Their modest height and compact shape (about 70 cm/28 in. tall and half as wide again), together with their easy care, make them splendid foliage plants for containers and confined gardens, for lining paths and entranceways, or for filling in difficult spots. *A. chathamica* has silvery green foliage and recurving leaves; *A. nervosa* has bluish green foliage; and a hybrid from the two species has succeeded in producing a bronze form. Astelias can take sun or shade, while adapting to almost any soil.

The New Zealand native *Aciphylla squarrosa*, the bayonet plant or spaniard, is not restricted to warm climates, growing equally well in cold areas. Although its spiky, yellow flowers enhance it in summer, it's the striking clump formation (around 1 m/3 ft high) that makes it ideal for the exotic garden. *A. squarrosa* can take full sun and some drought once mature, but because of its hazardously sharp sword points, it needs careful siting in the garden.

Another clumping sword-bearer is the huge spear lily or Gymea lily, *Doryanthes excelsa*. At maturity (which can take up to ten years), its succulent

Low-growing *Phormium* cultivars add a splash of colour to a tapestry of foliage textures, which includes young palms, papyrus and the large, dark green leaves of *Gunnera manicata*.

leaves can reach 1.2 m (4 ft) in length, numbering as many as a hundred, and it may produce an arching, 4 m (13 ft) flower-spike, the red blooms bunched at the tip and heavy with honey. It's a Queensland native, and while it likes warm, woodsy growing conditions, it makes such a commanding focal point that it needs to be positioned accordingly. *D. palmeri* has slightly ribbed leaves to 1.8 m (6 ft) and shorter, red flower-spikes (to 1 m/3 ft).

Statuesque succulents from drier climates, such as the aloes and agaves, come in a variety of dramatic and architectural forms, including clumping rosettes and whorls of sharp swords. The agaves are famous for their tall, tree-like flower-spikes, and the aloes are identified and popularised by the cure-all properties of a single species, *Aloe vera* (now *A. barbadensis*). Both have many species to choose from—the agaves about twenty and the aloes more than a hundred—and almost all are drought-tolerant. They are useful for filling dry spots in the garden, where their dramatic shape has instant impact.

The best-known agave is perhaps *Agave americana*, the century plant, which has a rosette of thick-fleshed, grey-green leaves that bend over from the middle. Its towering flower-stalk, up to 10 m (33 ft) tall with yellow flowers, will stop you in your tracks. *A. attenuata* is also a familiar accent plant, with its perfectly formed, light grey-green rosettes and an unusual flower-spike. Its gently arching tapers, fluffy with greenish yellow flowers, have earned it the name foxtail plant. As with all agaves, it is the foliage, not the flowering, that matters for the landscaper. The flowering represents the end of its cycle, the main rosette dying with the flower-stalk, leaving

Opposite, above: The eye-catching form of *Agave attenuata* dominates this garden, with two tall specimens of *Yucca aloifolia* showing the characteristic skirt of spent leaves.

Opposite: This garden of succulents features the stunning, yellow-flowered *Aloe thraskii* and an equally striking orange-flowered species.

This bold, sparsely planted landscape is dominated by the highly architectural forms of *Cycas revoluta* and *Agave attenuata*.

61

Opposite: The ponytail palm, *Beaucarnea recurvata*, is slow growing but can reach a height of about 8 m (26 ft) or so.

Opposite, below: One of the largest bromeliad species, *Bromelia balansae*, with its striking, bright red centre, deserves its common name of heart of fire.

Mature specimens of *Aloe arborescens* x *ferox* develop tall trunks. They are dramatic in flower, with spikes of vibrant orange-red.

behind offsets that will develop into new plants. *A. sisalana*, the agave cultivated for hemp, is similar to *A. americana*. *A. parviflora*, with white fibres peeling from the edges, grows to 1 m (3 ft). *A. filifera* grows to only 50 cm (20 in.), but its stalk of yellow-green flowers, produced in summer, can reach 2.5 m (8 ft). This species produces offsets very readily. *A. victoriae-reginae* forms a small (60 cm/24 in.) rosette, dense with white-edged, green leaves and very ornate. Other species include *A. albicans*, with cream variegation, and *A. angustifolia*, noted for its variegated form 'Marginata'. As all agaves have extremely sharp points in their armour, they should be sited with care. But since their bold shapes are most dramatic when viewed from a distance, or growing on an elevated site, their spikes are unlikely to be hidden from the unwary. Agaves are drought-tolerant but benefit from a bit of moisture and occasional manure.

A genus so similar that it could be mistaken for an agave is the less-common *Furcraea*. *F. foetida* (syn. *F. gigantea*), the giant false agave, is the largest species, with a rosette of broad, sword-shaped, green leaves. *F. selloa* var. *marginata* is a stunning sphere of daggers. The leaves are thin and flexible, up to 1 m (3 ft) long, and have yellow margins and sharp teeth.

Aloes come in all sizes, from miniature to massive, and many produce an annual crop of colourful candelabra in red, yellow and orange shades. Unlike agaves, aloes bloom annually and do not die after flowering. *Aloe arborescens*, one of the most familiar, has stems topped by rosettes of slender, tapering, dull blue-green leaves, and produces masses of bell-shaped, red flowers on long stalks. It grows to 3 m (10 ft). *A. africana* is similar, but the flowers are yellow with green tips. *A. barbadensis* (syn. *A. vera*) is lower growing, with thick, succulent leaves, and produces yellow flowers. *A. bainesii*, though a wonderful feature plant in the garden when young, eventually reaches tree size and becomes multi-trunked, with the succulent tufts of leaves confined to the outermost branch ends. It has salmon-pink flowers tipped with green. *A. marlothii* has especially thick leaves and bears brilliant yellow flowers on large flower-heads. *A. plicatilis* is distinctive for its rounded leaf ends—the rest of the family have skin-piercing points—as well as for its fan-like growth habit, which differs from the more usual rosette shape.

Among larger cacti that combine well with aloes and other succulents are columnar species, with their dramatic vertical shapes. *Espostoa lanata* is an extremely slow-growing, columnar cactus, which eventually reaches about 2 m (6.5 ft). Its fine 'wool' covering accounts for the name cotton ball cactus. *Cereus peruvianus* is a branching species, sharply ribbed, with short, golden spines on the columns of blue 'flesh'. It can reach a towering 5 m (16.5 ft). *Echinocactus grusonii* is spherical. Covered with golden wool and spines in perfect patterns, it grows on short stems to about 1 m (3 ft). All cacti, which are, of course, very drought-tolerant, benefit from compost and bone dust but have low nitrogen requirements. Too much nitrogen encourages rapid growth, which turns sappy and invites infection. With cacti, it's best to err on the side of neglect!

Among plants with architectural drama, there's nothing quite like *Beaucarnea recurvata*, the ponytail palm. It's not, in fact, a palm but a relation of the yuccas, and similarly xerophytic (adapted to the arid tropics). Beaucarnea's distinctive swollen base, which allows it to store a year-long supply of water, tapers to a smooth, palm-like trunk from which sprouts a dense, tufted rosette of ponytail leaves. These are long, very thin, and hang in slightly concave masses. *B. recurvata* is a splendid structural plant for a dry spot. Starting with a single trunk, which ultimately develops only a few palm-like branches, it is slow growing to about 8 m (26 ft). Apart from the need for occasional grooming, *B. recurvata* is wonderfully neglect-proof.

Several species of bromeliads are bold architectural plants. Most are low growing, but one that grows—and glows—above the rest is the astonishing *Bromelia balansae*. When the centre of the plant is emblazoned with scarlet, its common name of heart of fire is no overstatement. It has narrow, arching leaves edged with spines and, in spring and summer, bright red bracts.

The Japanese sago palm, *Cycas revoluta*, is one of the most commonly grown cycads. It requires conditions similar to palms but can withstand more sun, wind and drought.

The flower-head of the bromeliad *Puya alpestris* is a spectacular sight. This species is easy to grow and well suited to drier parts of the garden.

The genus *Puya* is another member of the *Bromeliaceae* family and includes several large and extraordinary species from South America's topographical extremes. These are terrestrial and inhabit high, arid deserts with fierce winds and even snow. The largest puya, *P. raimondii* (10 m/33 ft), which is also the largest of all bromeliads, is an unforgettable sight. Primordial like cycads, spiky like yuccas, drought-tolerant like cacti, rugged and virtually indestructible, *P. raimondii* lives for hundreds of years. *P. alpestris* is not as large but has a flower-head that is unique in the plant world. The *Illustrated London News* once attempted to describe it: 'Three-petalled goblets of waxy, silken texture of an unearthly blue-green . . . Standing up in the centre is a cluster of brilliant orange anthers, and in the middle of these is a tufted stigma of bright lettuce-green velvet.' This species is easy to grow, taking extremes of temperature in its stride, as well as long drought. Just make sure the drainage is swift—perhaps by growing it on rocks. *P. chilensis* is also large and dramatic, with flower-heads that are greenish yellow. All puyas need space and, like yuccas, cycads and large aloes, are seen to best advantage when they are uncrowded. Some puyas may reach 6 m (20 ft) across, and the flower-spikes can be enormous, while the individual spiny leaves that make up the rosette may number up to a hundred. Among bromeliads, puyas remain one of the easiest to grow—and they never need watering!

And now the aristocrats of all foliage plants—cycads. They are crown-like in appearance and royal in evolutionary terms; they can be traced back through the centuries and ice ages, unaltered, to primordial times. Primitive cycads reproduce through cone-like 'fruit', which distinguishes them from palms, with which they are usually associated. Cycads are a much older plant form. They are also lower growing, often with massive trunks; and their leaves, with one exception, are always pinnate or feathery, not palmate or hand-like. Their fronds are neatly and perfectly formed, and held in stiff symmetry around centres that draw attention like bull's-eyes. They're also slow growing, and those that do grow many metres high take about two hundred years to do so!

The best-known cycad species is probably *Cycas revoluta*, the Japanese sago palm. It's one of the most readily available and reliable to grow. *Encephalartos ferox* has deep green, feather-shaped leaves with broad, toothed leaflets, and colourful cones. *Macrozamia communis* and *M. moorei* are both native to Australia and grow to around 3 m (10 ft) tall, bearing sharp, narrow leaflets. *Lepidozamia peroffskyana* and *L. hopeii* are both very decorative; and *Zamia pumila* (syn. *Z. furfuracea*) from Mexico, while probably too tropical for most gardens, has highly textured, leathery leaflets. It is an ideal tub plant and will grow quite fast to about 50 cm (20 in.) tall.

Because cycads are not mass-produced like lettuce seedlings, obtaining them isn't always easy. To get the best selection, along with valuable advice, it's worth approaching a local palm and cycad society. On the whole, most species are fairly hardy. While their growing requirements are similar to those of palms (see page 28), they're generally tougher, able to withstand more sun, wind and drought than palms can. And if you're starting an exotic garden from scratch, undemanding cycads create wonderful focal points around which to design the rest of the layout.

The feathery fronds of this cycad contrast pleasingly with the sharp lines of the building.

Bamboo

Bamboo's place in the exotic garden is fundamental. For sharp, vertical, structural features, it is hard to beat. Its antiquity and ubiquity are renowned; its virtues are manifold, and its vices—in the form of underground runners—are easily avoided.

A plant of great energy, bamboo once recorded a growth rate of 1.2 m (4 ft) in 24 hours. It's also a plant of extraordinary grace: take a level, vacant spot in any garden, add a pot (or box, bowl or any container) in which is planted a bamboo clump arching to about 2 m (6.5 ft), and the result is a screen of elegant, vertical lines softened with graceful and airy, green filaments. It's true that neglected and undernourished specimens can look tired and scruffy and not warrant a second glance, but well-cared-for bamboo, like that grown by true enthusiasts, is a different matter. Such people take sharp tools to old clumps and remove every dead stick, grooming the foliage as they go. Some even polish the canes.

Bamboo species—many of which belong to the genus *Bambusa*, a name derived from the Malay common name 'bambu'—can be divided into two kinds according to the manner in which the plants increase. Clumping bamboos increase sympodially—that is, new culms or stems sprout from the underground rhizome within the clump or at its periphery. These are the desirable species for the garden. In the second group, the running bamboos or monopodials, the rhizome bolts away underground, intent on reaching the furthest point by the straightest route in the shortest possible time, where it then breaks ground with incredible vigour, instantly at home in its new surroundings. This group is too invasive and should not be planted in the home garden—except, perhaps, on an island in the middle of a pond or lake, since bamboos can't survive water or waterlogged soil. In defence of these monopodials, it should be pointed out that in their original habitats, on high slopes and in earthquake-prone areas of Japan and mainland Asia, they perform valuable erosion control, and their formidably extensive subterranean networks are able to withstand earthquakes perfectly. The species and cultivars described below, however, are all clumping, not running.

All the small to medium-sized bamboos grow splendidly in containers. This allows them to be positioned in different places for different effects, according to weather, season or light, or to be moved from beside a pool when leaves are being shed excessively, usually in late summer. Growing bamboo in containers is a useful way of creating privacy on a deck or balcony—two or three containers together can create a dense barrier. One distinct benefit of growing bamboo in a container is that it does not compete with other plants in the garden. Bamboos are hungry feeders and tend to rob the surrounding soil of nutrition and moisture.

A container needs to be deep (ideally, one-fifth of the plant's height) and tapered for ease of repotting. It will, of course, have drainage holes, and a holding tray underneath is beneficial. Commercially available planter mixes for shrubs have enough nutrients to last about six months, after which

The bare stems of this clump of *Bambusa oldhamii* can be as attractive as the foliage—and bamboo clumps are self-mulching.

The elegant *Bambusa gracilis* grows in tidy clumps and is an ideal bamboo for small gardens. Note the variegated foliage of a lower-growing species on the right of the path.

supplements are needed. Seaweed and fish extracts are excellent, and slow-release fertilisers add nutrients in the right proportions. Containers need daily moisture. If possible, allow them all the rain that falls, and when it's not raining, water by hand. Don't rely on overhead sprinklers, because the density of the plant may prevent the roots from getting a good soaking. Bamboos relish humidity and will benefit from an occasional misting. With careful watering and feeding, they can grow and flourish for years in the same container. When a plant eventually outgrows the container, it can be turned out, and the roots and foliage reduced to half, before being returned to the same container, with fresh soil, or repotted in something bigger. Container-grown bamboos are very easy to care for and rarely suffer from pests or disease.

As a waterside plant—but not in waterlogged soil—bamboo is ideal. Here, *Bambusa gracilis* overhangs a handsome *Gunnera manicata*.

In the ground, bamboo needs space. Allow for its maximum height and leave ample room for the clump to spread. Remember that even the non-running species are devilish to dig out should you ever decide to do so. Bamboos like humus and a high organic content, but are not too fussy about the pH level. Sharp drainage is essential; water-retentive clay is fatal. They prefer full sun but will grow well in quarter-shade or even half-shade. (To keep bamboo alive but not increasing in size, plant it in full shade.) When planting a bamboo hedge, dig a continuous trench to encourage growth between plants.

There are many species of bamboo, not all of which will be readily available in garden centres. Gardeners seeking particular species, or very rare ones, should contact a local bamboo society. One small (3 m/10 ft) garden favourite is the serene *Bambusa gracilis* (syn. *Chimonobambusa falcata*), with very slender stems and narrow, fresh leaves. The topmost portion arches gracefully, especially after rain. It forms a neat clump, is cold-tolerant and rarely needs trimming. In a shaded site, which it prefers, the culms will be covered in a powdery, bluish bloom. After flowering (once in fifteen years), the plant usually dies. *B. gracilis* grows well in containers. There are several cultivars, including a lighter, more yellow-stemmed variety and a darker-stemmed one, as well as a bushier, lower-growing plant.

Drepanostachyum falcatum has thin, arching stems like *Bambusa gracilis* and grows to about the same height. The stems are a dark olive-green and the

leaves bright emerald-green.

Bambusa 'Wong Tsai' is a small, slender cultivar whose stems, if left untrimmed, arch out and down in fountain form; the leaves are slightly curly. 'Wong Tsai' does well in a container and is recommended for planting by patios and buildings. Like 'Wong Tsai', *Bambusa ventricosa* is suitable for a container, though in its native China it may reach 10 m (33 ft) or more. Its common name is Buddha's belly bamboo, because of its swollen internodes, most in evidence when the plant is pot-grown. Although unlikely to be a first choice as a garden feature, it's a good species for screening. *Bambusa ventricosa* 'Tegens' is a drought-resistant plant with green stems that arch outwards quite near the ground—making it one of the widest-growing 'fountain' clumps.

The largest of the giant bamboos is *Dendrocalamus giganteus*, the famous tropical titan whose 25 cm (10 in.), wood-walled culms have for centuries been used to build bridges and temples in Asia. In the hot tropics it reaches more than 30 m (100 ft) tall. *D. latiflorus* is a magnificent upright bamboo with deep green leaves 30 cm (12 in.) long. It's one of the best non-suckering species to grow if you want drama and impact in a large garden. It reaches a height of 12 m (40 ft) or more, and needs a warm, sheltered site and abundant moisture. *D. hookerii* is another medium to large species that grows well in the subtropics.

Bambusa oldhamii is a more moderate-sized plant of neat appearance, widely grown as a reliable hedge. Planted singly, it's effective too—the 18 cm (7 in.) leaves are wide and dark green, the clump very upright and dense, growing to 9 m (30 ft) or more.

Bambusa multiplex (syn. *B. glaucescens*) is an upright bamboo, to about 12 m (40 ft), and is often used for hedges and windbreaks. The cultivar 'Silverstripe' (to 10 m/33 ft) has the stems and foliage decoratively variegated with creamy white stripes. Another striped cultivar, 'Alphonse Karr', has long been a popular ornamental, valued for its orange-pink stems with vertical green stripes. The clump has a rounded, bushy shape when mature and grows to about 6 m (20 ft). *Bambusa multiplex* var. *riviereorum*, Chinese goddess bamboo, is really miniature. It grows slowly to only 2 m (6.5 ft), sometimes less, but never more than 3 m (10 ft), and its very slender stems lined with thin, lance-shaped leaves bend appealingly. It's a choice variety worth growing well; give it very rich, slightly acid soil, moisture and, above all, shelter. It is at its best when grown up against a wall.

Bambusa vulgaris is one of the most widely grown of all bamboos. It is found extensively in Southeast Asia as well as in Central and South America and tropical Africa. It's a large, robust plant, with arching stems reaching up to 20 m (66 ft) in the hot tropics but usually under 10 m (33 ft) in the subtropics. The lustre of the stems is more apparent in this species because the dark green leaves—contrasting with the golden yellow of the ageing stems—grow from the upper portion of the culm only. *B. vulgaris* needs a warm, sheltered spot to grow well.

Imaginative landscapers find bamboos exciting plants to use in designs where the vertical lines can contrast with horizontal ones—decking on several levels, for example, retaining walls built of horizontal timber, or level paving.

The bright green foliage of a healthy *Drepanostachyum falcatum* screens this building. The red flowers of *Metrosideros collina* 'Tahiti' provide an attractive contrast.

One of the most effective locations of all is beside water, especially where reflection doubles the impact. Since bamboos cannot tolerate wet feet, their positioning and need for drainage, as well as their habit of shedding leaves, should be taken into account. In small gardens, containers may be the solution.

Because bamboos have had such long histories in their places of origin compared with their recent short period of attention by Western botanists, their taxonomy is particularly prone to confusion. Bamboo societies and individual collectors are doing their best to simplify multiple naming and impose uniformity, so don't be put off by inconsistencies. Find species that appeal, site and plant them appropriately, enjoy their vigour, and see them add architecture to your garden.

Tree Ferns

Tree ferns also symbolise lush rainforests. There are two main genera: *Cyathea* and *Dicksonia*, with a choice of a dozen or so species of the former and a half-dozen species of the latter. All have the same requirements: plenty of shade when young, slightly acid, humus-rich soil, and moisture in abundance. Unlike smaller fern species, tree ferns can tolerate periods of drought in later life, but only when fully mature and well established.

Cyathea arborea, the West Indian tree fern, can reach 7 m (23 ft) or more and is distinguished by its light colour—a yellowy green. The trunk is slender and the fronds frilly. Coming from the tropics, it naturally prefers warmth. *C. dregei* is a smaller species, slow growing to 2–3 m (6.5–10 ft), with a stout trunk and deep green fronds. *C. australis*, the Australian rough tree fern, native to Norfolk Island and Australia, is at home in a subtropical to temperate climate and is relatively cold-hardy. In cooler climates it tolerates exposure to sun; in hotter areas it needs more shade. *C. australis* is popularly grown as a garden and container plant; its tidy, 2 m (6.5 ft) long fronds and height to 4 m (13 ft) make it a useful and not overwhelming size for many gardens. *C. brownii*, native to Norfolk Island, is vigorous when young and grows to a tall 6 m (20 ft).

Cyathea australis, an adaptable, undemanding tree fern, forms the main feature of this shady fernery.

Splashes of colour are provided by impatiens and bromeliads among the tree ferns and bamboo edging this path. The trunks of *Dicksonia squarrosa* show their conspicuous woody texture.

If you're in a hurry and it's fast growth you want, *Cyathea cunninghamii*, at least in its native New Zealand, will perform with greater speed than most other species. It reaches a maximum height of around 3.5 m (11.5 ft), with a relatively small crown of fronds, and is fussy in its requirements: an acid, humus-rich soil is essential, while sun and wind are both harmful. *C. medullaris*, the black tree fern or mamaku, on the other hand, a tall-growing species native to New Zealand, is less fussy about conditions and very adaptable. However, it is not as appealing in appearance as many other tree ferns, if only because its rough, black trunk carries the fronds to such a towering height (up to 6 m/20 ft or more). *C. dealbata*, the silver fern or ponga, has attractive silvery undersides to the fronds. While its crown develops quickly, the trunk is slow to grow but eventually reaches about 3 m (10 ft)—a useful landscaping height.

Cyathea medullaris, or black ponga, is at home in any subtropical garden.

Cyathea cooperi is a little less modest in size, reaching an ultimate height of 3–5 m (10–16.5 ft). It's one of the most commonly grown species, as it adapts to many situations, including sun, as long as water is plentiful. *C. cooperi* is noted for its decorative, lacy fronds and the texture on its trunk (formed by old fronds), known as 'coin spotting'. *C. smithii* is native to New Zealand's cooler regions and really grows best when out of the subtropics. Its large fronds are soft and bright green, and it reaches up to 6 m (20 ft).

Cyathea robusta is a 2–4 m (6.5–13 ft) tall, shade-loving fern from Lord Howe Island. But the loveliest has been kept till last: the rare and prized *C. kermadecensis*, from the Kermadec Islands. It grows to a little over 3 m (10 ft), needs high humidity and plenty of moisture, and holds its dark green fronds at right angles to the trunk. Its fellow Kermadec Islander, *C. milnii*, is equally appealing. Both are unlikely to be found in garden centres, however, and will need to be obtained from specialist nurseries.

Of the dicksonias, *Dicksonia antarctica*, the Australian soft tree fern, is widely grown around the world, especially in cool temperate areas, which it prefers to warmer regions. Its crown of fronds is dark and characteristically very dense, bearing a greater number of individual fronds than most other tree ferns, and the 1–4 m (3–13 ft) trunk is robust and very fibrous. *D. antarctica* is particularly popular with landscapers because even mature specimens are easily transplanted. *D. fibrosa*, the New Zealand native wheki-ponga, also favours cooler conditions. It grows to no more than 4 m (13 ft) and has as its distinguishing feature a 'skirt' of old fronds curtaining the very fibrous trunk. *D. lantana* is very unusual and little known. Like *D. fibrosa*, it is native to New Zealand, but unlike other tree ferns its habit is almost prostrate (to 2 m/6.5 ft). *D. squarrosa*, or wheki, yet another New Zealander, is a clumping tree fern with fronds that are harsh and prickly but held in graceful arches from the slender trunk, making it a very ornamental garden feature. And lastly, *D. sellowiana*, from Central and South America, produces narrow, dark green fronds from slender trunks and is a handsome, 2–4 m (6.5–13 ft) tree fern when given full shade and moisture.

Above, left: *Dicksonia squarrosa*, with their crowns of graceful, spreading fronds, are an important structural feature in this garden.

Flowering Trees

Below: The Illawarra flame tree, *Brachychiton acerifolius*, has clusters of bright scarlet flowers in spring and summer.

Bottom: The Mexican hand tree, *Chiranthodendron pentadactylon*, is admired for its unusual, hand-like flowers and attractive foliage.

From around the Pacific rim and from countries bordering the Indian Ocean comes a collection of flowering trees with spectacular blooms in high-voltage colours, as befits the tropics. Some, however, grow to be so large that they're unsuitable for small gardens, though they would make magnificent specimens in parks or in gardens on the rural-urban fringes where space is less limited. But these spreading, well-anchored, robust trees are so brilliant in flower that it would be a shame to bypass them on account of their ultimate size, so here's a suggestion for compromise. A number of them can be grown well and will even flower well in containers, and there are advantages in growing them this way for the first few years. Containers can be moved around, allowing those trees that are fully tropical in origin, and not from stock that has proved itself over generations outside the tropics, to be moved to a sheltered site (such as a porch) in winter. For eight or nine months of the year in the subtropics such trees will be fine, but there will be times when an unexpected chill could be fatal to young plants in the ground. By moving the tub to a warm spot, the tree's hardening-off process can be controlled. Keep this up until the tree is a couple of metres high. The longer it's cared for in the pot, the more resistant it's likely to be when planted out.

First, here is a selection of the best very big flowering trees, chosen from a large number that could equally well grace a subtropical garden but aren't quite as brilliant. Following on from these—all of which grow to over 10 m (33 ft), some topping 20 m (66 ft)—comes a survey of smaller flowering trees, which, while in some instances capable of reaching maximum heights of 8 m (26 ft), are mostly much smaller than this.

Here are some outstanding red-flowering species for a start. Bright colours are meant for bright light. The same red that in a misty, northern light might seem garish can be seductively glamorous under a tropical or subtropical sun. The Illawarra flame tree, *Brachychiton acerifolius*, a celebrated native of subtropical New South Wales and Queensland, has this kind of fire. It shares with other subtropical and tropical species the habit of shedding its leaves in early summer for the duration of its flowering. Both leaves and flowers make a good display: the scarlet flowers hang in clusters; the leaves are glossy and deeply lobed. The tree is variable in size and regularity of flowering. Other brachychitons include *B. gregorii*, the desert kurrajong, from Africa, and the huge tropical Queensland bottle tree, *B. rupestris*, which has an intriguing, swollen, bottle-shaped trunk, up to 3.5 m (11.5 ft) in diameter, functioning as a reservoir for storing water. All brachychitons do well in dryish climates. Their heights at maturity vary from 12 to 20 m (40–66 ft).

Chiranthodendron pentadactylon is the Mexican hand tree, admired for its unusual, hand-like flowers in deep rich red. These appeal as much to florists as to nectar-feeding birds. Though it flowers almost all year round in the tropics, in the subtropics it's likely to do so in spring and early summer. It has large, heart-shaped, lobed leaves, and in rich soil with plenty of water it's fast growing to 25 m (82 ft) or more.

Metrosideros excelsa needs no introduction in New Zealand, where its status as the pre-eminent coastal tree is embodied in the common name pohutukawa, Maori for 'drenched with salt spray'. As well as being tolerant of sea air, it tolerates drought and wind, produces nectar for bees and birds, and is an arresting sight in summer. The flowers, composed mostly of long stamens, are a dazzling deep crimson. The evergreen leaves are dark green with white felted undersides, and its ultimate spread is usually twice as wide as its ultimate height, which may be anywhere from 10 to 20 m (33–66 ft).

Although *Butea monosperma* (syn. *B. frondosa*) comes from tropical Burma and Bangladesh, where it is known as the flame of the forest, it's not as confined to tropical conditions as might be supposed. Given attentive nurturing, with a hardening-off period as it develops, a mature tree may well prove as resistant to cold as it has to coastal and saline conditions. Treat it well and it will respond by producing large clusters of glistening, orange-red flowers. A deciduous species, with bluish grey leaves following the flowers, *B. monosperma* grows very slowly to around 10 m (33 ft).

The large clan of erythrinas offers a variety of sizes, from tall trees to shrubs, all deciduous, and with the equally varied red flowers appearing against bare branches. Most species have thorns, and, on the whole, they like slightly drier conditions than other subtropicals. One of the largest is *Erythrina sykesii*, which can reach about 14 m (46 ft). It is widely grown for its coral flowers in winter and early spring. Other large species include *E. caffra* (12–14 m/40-46 ft) and *E. vespertilio* (8 m/26 ft).

The pohutukawa or New Zealand Christmas tree, *Metrosideros excelsa*, is well suited to dry and coastal conditions.

75

Equally flamboyant and equally at home in a dry, warm garden is the modest-sized parrot tree or tree fuchsia, *Schotia brachypetala*. In spring it sheds its leaves just before putting on a vibrant show of deep crimson flowers, which in its native Transvaal and in northern Australia attract parrots. Such is the lure of the nectar that the birds can become intoxicated. *S. brachypetala* is useful for dry areas, as it is thoroughly drought-tolerant. It is slow growing to about 12 m (40 ft).

The next two species are both brilliant, red-flowered aristocrats of the tropical world. They're from equatorial regions and must have a hot micro-climate to succeed. Grow them in containers during their infancy and juvenile stage, and after hardening off, plant them in the warmest possible location and nurture them well. The effort will be worthwhile. *Delonix regia*, the royal poinciana tree, sheds its feathery leaves to explode in summer with vibrant red flowers, each up to 10 cm (4 in.) long. The flowers are followed by long, hanging pods. At around 10 m (33 ft) high at maturity and with a much wider spread—up to 15 m (50 ft)—it's not surprising that the botanical name *Delonix*, from the Greek 'delos', means 'obvious'.

Spathodea campanulata, the African tulip tree, also glows like fire when in flower. A member of the *Bignoniaceae* family, it has pinnate foliage and lusciously bell-shaped, frilly-edged, orange-vermillion flowers, which face upwards with the frills etched in yellow—a lovely sight! It reaches a mature height of about 15 m (50 ft) and is very vulnerable to strong winds. (Spathodea shares its other common name of flame of the forest with *Butea monosperma*.)

The Australian flowering gum, *Eucalyptus ficifolia*, is another drought-tolerant tree with showy flowers.

Stenocarpus sinuatus is an Australian native flame tree. A narrow, upright tree, to 12 m (40 ft) or more, with glossy, lance-shaped leaves, *S. sinuatus* acquired its popular name Queensland firewheel tree because its scarlet flowers with prominent stamens are arranged in clusters like the spokes of a wheel. It's a member of the *Proteaceae* family and therefore needs acid, well-drained soil free of chemicals. (Herbicides, especially, should be avoided as any weed-spraying within 10 m/33 ft can kill it.)

Can any list of flowering trees omit Australia's glorious gums? *Eucalyptus ficifolia*, from Western Australia, ignites its blaze in spring and summer, a mass of stamen clusters amid the evergreen leaves. Shades range from pale pink to deep red—and all are stunning. A drought-tolerant species, *E. ficifolia* grows fairly fast from seedling stage to 10 m (33 ft).

Buckinghamia celsissima is another Australian native with panicles of sweetly fragrant, ivory flowers resembling bottle-brush flowers. It has a compact growth habit, to about 12 m (40 ft), and is a popular garden tree throughout New South Wales and Queensland. In its early life it is best grown in partial shade, and it should be pruned to encourage a single trunk.

One of the most celebrated subtropical flowering trees (also claimed by Australia but in fact native to Brazil) is *Jacaranda mimosifolia*. In bloom, both the tree and the ground beneath become a blur of lavender-blue. The deciduous jacaranda grows to about 10 m (33 ft) tall with a spread of about

Jacaranda mimosifolia is a stunning sight in full bloom. Here it is complemented by the versatile *Trachelospermum jasminoides*, or star jasmine, which can be grown as a climber or ground cover.

Chorisia speciosa, the floss silk tree, has a distinctive, thorn-studded trunk.

Top: *Lagerstroemia indica*, one of the crepe myrtles, flowers profusely in summer.

6 m (20 ft). It needs protection from cold winds and prefers a dryish soil once mature.

A pink-flowering tree, but with the peculiarity of never bearing flowers of exactly the same shade from one tree to the next, is *Chorisia speciosa*, also from Brazil. Floss silk tree, its common name, sounds innocent enough, and refers to the silky floss on the seeds, but the thorns are far from silky; they're brutally sharp and studded over the entire trunk. *C. speciosa* is semi-deciduous, with its hibiscus-like flowers appearing in late autumn or early winter. It grows best in a fairly sweet soil. Another less-common species, *C. insignis*, the white floss silk tree, has large, lily-like, creamy-white flowers. Chorisias develop very thick trunks and reach an ultimate height of around 12 m (40 ft).

Calodendrum capense, the Cape chestnut, another pink-flowering ornamental, grows best in the company of other trees. Though it needs plenty of water at all times—being not at all drought-tolerant—it's worth growing for its flowers. These are highly fragrant, rhododendron-like, in soft pink with spidery stamens—most elegant. *C. capense* is evergreen to semi-deciduous, rapid growing given enough moisture, and has a maximum height of about 16 m (52 ft).

The crepe myrtles, *Lagerstroemia*, of which there are some fifty species native to Asia and the western Pacific, all flower gorgeously in pinkish shades, from pale salmon to rich rosy-mauve. *L. speciosa*, the rose of India, is a deciduous species well known for its clusters of funnel-shaped, crinkly, mauve or purple to rose flowers. While unlikely to reach its 20 m (66 ft) height in the subtropics, *L. speciosa* is probably the pick of them all, although appealing new hybrids and cultivars, especially in dwarf sizes, are becoming increasingly available. *L. indica* is smaller than *L. speciosa* and is often grown as a shrub. Its attractive flower-heads consist of white, pink or purple flowers with crinkled, crepe-like petals. As crepe myrtles flower on new wood, pruning encourages flowering. They need good shelter and watering.

The tabebuias are exuberant flowering trees. All told, there are about seventy of them; some are small, while others grow to towering heights. Their glory is the generous clusters of trumpet flowers, which are among the largest and showiest of all flowering trees. *Tabebuia rosea* (syn. *T. penta-phylla*), the pink trumpet tree, is usually evergreen, although deciduous in cool climates. It has pink flowers in spring and grows rapidly to 18 m (60 ft) or more. *T. chrysotricha*, the golden trumpet tree, is less common and more tender, growing to about 10 m (33 ft). It has dark green leaves divided into leaflets and rich yellow flowers borne in late winter or early spring. The leaves and stems are covered with golden hairs. Given warmth and deep, rich soil, tabebuias will flower when quite young.

Hymenosporum flavum, the Australian frangipani, is a tall evergreen tree—not overwhelming in a small garden because it doesn't become massive. It has panicles of tubular flowers that are cream at first and become more yellow as they age. Hymenosporum is renowned for its exquisite scent, tantalising from many metres away. One of the most fragrant of all trees, it's a treasure. (A new dwarf form has recently become available; see page 108).

For really large and lavish yellow flowers, try growing *Cochlospermum vitifolium*, the buttercup tree. However, as well as being difficult to obtain, it's a tropical species and needs nurturing. The glistening, cup-sized blooms, which last for three months against the bare branches, and which can appear on even very young trees, are highly ornamental. It's a deciduous species, with lobed, toothed leaves up to 30 cm (12 in.) across. Drought-tolerant at maturity, *C. vitifolium* rarely exceeds 10 m (33 ft).

Another yellow beauty that's hard to obtain, and therefore mentioned only in passing, is *Peltophorum pterocarpum* (syn. *P. ferrugineum*), the yellow flame tree. It's a handsome tree with luxuriant, feathery foliage and rust-red buds opening into sizzling yellow-orange, fragrant flowers. Dark red pods remain on the tree until the following flowering season.

Tipuana tipu is a broad, spreading tree, which should be sited in full sun with protection from strong winds. It's fast growing to around 14 m (46 ft) or more and has fresh green, fern-like leaves. But it's the profuse sprays of golden, pea-like flowers that make this tree so noteworthy and have earned it the common name of pride of Bolivia.

Barklya syringifolia, the gold blossom tree, bears its golden orange flowers in stiff upright sprays, which make a striking display. It's evergreen, with deep green, heart-shaped leaves resembling those of the lilac, as the name suggests. Though native to Queensland rainforests and needing warmth and moisture, barklyas seem surprisingly cold-tolerant (to 0°C) and have been grown successfully in southern Europe. In favourable conditions this tree will reach 14 m (46 ft).

There is one subtropical tree that is outstanding in every way: the

The Australian frangipani, *Hymenosporum flavum*, has sweetly fragrant flowers that are cream at first but become yellow with age. In the foreground is a handsome specimen of *Fatsia japonica*.

Left: The hanging racemes of flowers on the macadamia are as attractive as its glossy, leathery leaves.

Right: The pea-like flowers of *Castanospermum australe*, the Moreton Bay chestnut, are well hidden among the foliage.

Bauhinia purpurea has orchid-like flowers typical of the genus.

macadamia. It has pleasing form and dense foliage of glossy, dark green, leathery leaves; it's fast growing; it can be used as a windbreak; its hanging racemes of starry, stamened flowers are long and decorative—they scent the air with honey sweetness; and mature trees bear, by the barrowload, nuts considered by many to be the choicest eating nuts in the world. There are two species: *Macadamia integrifolia* and *M. tetraphylla*. The latter has especially attractive new foliage, bright pink in spring, and the nuts have twice the sugar content of *M. integrifolia*. However, *M. integrifolia* is grown commercially because the nuts are produced over a longer period, are smoother and rounder in shape, and are better for roasting. 'Beaumont', a hybrid of the two species, is a reliable self-fertile variety that crops well. Trees take five or six years to bear, but grafted trees will produce nuts in three or four years. Best results come from planting in a warm, sheltered spot with day-long sun, using plenty of compost at planting time and mulching thereafter. Macadamias need excellent drainage.

Other large flowering trees that will produce an impressive display in the subtropical garden include: *Caesalpinia ferrea*, *Xanthostemon chrysanthus*, and *Castanospermum australe*.

Now to the smaller flowering trees. These don't reach the massive proportions at maturity of those described above, and many of them lend themselves to trimming and shaping. Thirty or so species are listed here, all of which are impressive in flower.

Bauhinias are a joy, famous for their orchid-like flowers. An average-sized city garden is likely to have room for two or more. Unlike ornamental flowering cherries, which have a burst of blossom in spring, bauhinias flower for many months of the year. Generally, the warmer the location, the longer the flowering period. To get the best display, give them a warm, open site in full sun, in fertile soil with a good mulch; waterlogged soil is fatal. For the first few years they're vulnerable to winter chills; after that they seem to toughen up.

Bauhinia blakeana, the Hong Kong orchid tree, is evergreen, to 4 m (13 ft), with large, divided leaves. Its showy orchid flowers are rose–purple. *B. variegata*, the purple orchid tree, is evergreen or semi-deciduous, to 5 m (16.5 ft), with oval, deeply notched leaves. The fragrant flowers are carmine with a deep purple stripe and shaped like a cattleya orchid. *B. variegata* 'Candida', the white orchid tree, has fragrant, pure white flowers up to 10 cm (4 in.) across. It grows to 6 m (20 ft). *B. purpurea*, evergreen and spreading to about 3 m (10 ft), has fragrant, deep purple flowers throughout spring and summer. *B. retusa* has very showy, bright yellow blooms; *B. monandra*, the pink orchid (4 m/13 ft), is perhaps the showiest of them all, with very large, profuse orchid blooms, pale salmon splashed with deep red.

Another group of small trees noted for their stunning flowers is the sub-tropical dombeyas, often collectively known as Natal cherry trees. They are easy to grow, becoming more drought-tolerant as they mature, and they make good cut flowers. Dombeyas prefer full sun and fertile, well-drained soil. When flowering is finished, the brown calyxes usually stay on the stems—if this seems a dull encore after a lavish performance, remove them by hand or prune the tree. *Dombeya cacuminum*, from Madagascar, has red flowers that don't stay on the branches when flowering finishes.

D. tiliacea (syn. *D. natalensis*), the Natal cherry or heartleaf dombeya, has

Dombeya 'Pink Clouds' is an attractive small tree that bears a profusion of flowers in autumn.

The frangipani, *Plumeria rubra*, will grow in a container or in the garden—the warmer the site, the better. It bears its highly scented flowers in summer.

beautiful, fragrant, white blooms in winter. It is a spreading, evergreen tree, reaching 3–8 m (10–26 ft). *D. spectabilis* (3 m/10 ft) has pale pink or creamy white flowers in early spring and is slightly more cold-tolerant. It is semi-evergreen, and the flowers often appear on leafless branches. *D. wallichii* has pink flowers and reaches 8 m (26 ft) or more, while *D. cayeuxii*, a smaller, shrubby tree, has fragrant, rose-pink blooms.

From the Natal cherry to its South American counterpart, the Brazilian cherry: *Eugenia uniflora* (syn. *Syzygium uniflora*), also known as the Surinam cherry, has glossy leaves and sweetly scented, white flowers in clusters preceding small, piquant, edible fruits. It grows to about 6 m (20 ft) and needs a warm, humid site.

Scented white flowers of a much larger size appear in winter on the fast-growing, evergreen to semi-evergreen *Michelia doltsopa*. This is a pleasing pyramidal tree (to 10 m/33 ft) and a close relative of magnolias; it grows easily provided the soil is acid and moist, is tolerant of light frosts and is best in half-shade, at least in its early years.

Radermacheria sinensis also bears fragrant, creamy flowers. Long popular as a house plant under the name of Canton lace plant, it is aptly named: its small, deep green leaves spread in a network of filigree, making it a superb foliage plant. Though capable of growing into a large tree in the tropics, in the subtropics it is likely to reach only 7 m (23 ft).

The most celebrated of all tropical flowers, the fragrant frangipani, grows throughout the Pacific, and with nurturing can be grown and will flower successfully in subtropical regions. *Plumeria rubra* has, as anyone who has ever smelt it knows, a rich, seductive scent. In the tropics the tree may exceed 10 m (33 ft), but in the subtropics it is unlikely to reach more than 4 m (13 ft) with a wider spread. The tree is deciduous, and its many branches are fleshy and rather graceless when bare, but this can be forgiven in a plant with such exquisite perfume. The leaves are pointed and dark green, and the waxy, single flowers, in shades of red, pink, orange and yellow, appear in summer. *P. rubra* needs rich soil, ample water and high humidity in summer, and shelter from strong winds at all times. And, of course, the warmer the site, the better it does. It grows and flowers well in containers, and it strikes easily from cuttings taken in late summer—plant it under a sunny window! In tropical Asia the white-flowered species *P. obtusa* is known as the temple flower or pagoda tree. The leaves are up to 18 cm (7 in.) long, and the intensely fragrant, white flowers with yellow centres, up to 8 cm (3.5 in.) across, occur in summer; this species does not grow as well in higher latitudes.

Tabebuia argentea, the silver trumpet tree, is one of the smaller-growing species in this large genus, up to 8 m (26 ft) tall and well worth growing. It is deciduous, with silvery grey leaves, and the golden yellow trumpet flowers appear in spring on leafless branches. *T. chrysantha*, the Venezuelan golden trumpet tree, grows to 4 m (13 ft) and produces tubular, yellow flowers over a long period.

Tecoma stans (syn. *Bignonia stans*) commonly known as yellow bells, is another yellow—though deeper golden—flowering evergreen of pleasing upright shape (to about 5 m/16.5 ft). It can be kept smaller by pruning. It has a profusion of funnel-shaped, yellow flowers throughout summer and autumn.

Sophora microphylla is a yellow-flowering native of Chile and New Zealand (kowhai), with very small and very fine, feathery leaves and a slightly weeping habit. The bright yellow flowers hang along its branches in spring and attract nectar-feeding birds. *S. tetraptera* is a larger-growing species (to 10 m/33 ft), and the cultivar 'Gnome' is a small form useful in small gardens, growing to only 2.5 m (8 ft). Sophoras grow well in both half-shade and full sun. *S. secundiflora*, the mescal bean, is a violet-flowered relative, native to Mexico and the southern United States. It is a neat, evergreen tree, up to 5 m (16.5 ft) tall, with pea-like flowers in drooping clusters in late spring. The flowers have a distinct violet scent.

Bolusanthus speciosus, the tree wisteria, from South Africa, is a slow-growing, deciduous tree, to 5 m (16.5 ft), with glossy, green leaves appearing after the flowers. These are purple and pea-like, and are borne in pendulous racemes in autumn. *Rhodoleia championii*, a bushy, evergreen tree with the

Alberta magna: on the left is the orange flower and on the right the scarlet calyx that follows.

common name of Hong Kong rose, reaches 4 m (13 ft) or so. It has glossy, bright green, leathery leaves and bears insignificant flowers in attractive, rosy pink bracts in late winter.

Alberta magna is a small tree or large shrub from South Africa, grown for its shiny, very dark green leaves, rather like laurel leaves, and for its clusters of orange-red flowers. Densely evergreen and flowering over a long period, *A. magna* requires plenty of water in summer and will grow (to 4 m/13 ft) in full sun or semi-shade. It's a tree that is always neat and compact.

Bixa orellana, the lipstick tree or annatto tree, is an evergreen with smooth, heart-shaped leaves up to 18 cm (7 in.) long. It has reddish pink flowers and fleshy fruit from which the yellowish red dye annatto is derived. It's fairly tender, being native to the West Indies, but given a hot spot it will reach up to 8 m (26 ft). It's bushy and fairly fast growing, and can be encouraged as a tree or a shrub.

Sesbania tripetii, the scarlet wisteria or glory pea, a native of Argentina, is valued for its quickly achieved but long-lasting summer raiment of orange-scarlet, pea-like flowers in pendulous racemes. It's a fast-growing, small treelet, reaching 3 m (10 ft), and is quite cold-tolerant; unfortunately it is short-lived. It is evergreen, with long, pinnate, dark green leaves.

Several small-growing species of *Erythrina* bring vivid splashes of colour to the garden. *E. crista-galli*, the cockscomb coral tree, has rich crimson 'cockscomb' flowers in racemes up to 50 cm (20 in.) long, occurring in several crops annually. It is deciduous, and the leaves, which consist of three oval leaflets, occur on prickly stems. *E. speciosa* (syn. *E. polianthes*, *E. reticulata*) is also deciduous, growing to about 4 m (13 ft), and produces striking racemes of brilliant crimson flowers in spring, before the leaves appear.

Similarly hued, though perhaps more orange, the flowers of *Cordia sebestena*, the geiger tree, flame for long periods in summer. This is a small, evergreen tree, to 8 m (26 ft), with much to recommend it. It has dark green, oval leaves and brilliant orange flowers, with frilled and crepe-like petals, which occur in racemes in summer. These are followed by small edible berries.

Opposite, above: *Erythrina crista-galli*, the cockscomb coral tree, produces these spectacular flowers in summer and autumn.

Opposite: Cassias are synonymous with warm-climate gardens, providing a bright display for much of the year.

84

And finally, in this brief survey of small trees, there's that well-known group of cheerful tropical and subtropical species, the cassias, plants that straddle any arbitrary division of shrubs and trees. Most cassias are indeed shrubs (see page 107), but a few are small trees. There's nothing meagre about cassia flowers. They burst forth from budding racemes into profuse displays of sulphur-yellow or pale lemon, salmon or deep gold through to ochre red. What's more, they flower for months on end. Of the four to five hundred species, the largest, *Cassia grandis*, the pink shower tree, can grow to 15 m (50 ft) in a favourable environment, though in the subtropics it is unlikely to exceed 8 m (26 ft). It's deciduous, with fern-like leaves that are covered in a fine down. In early summer it produces clusters of salmon-pink flowers. *C. marksiana* is similar to *C. grandis* but with brilliant yellow flowers. *C. spectabilis*, the popcorn bush, has long, pinnate leaves with bright green leaflets and bears erect racemes of shining gold flowers. The flowers of *C. occidentalis* are mahogany-red. *C. fistula*, the golden shower or Indian laburnum, bears its fragrant, bright yellow blooms in drooping racemes, like bunches of grapes. It's deciduous and grows rapidly to about 6 m (20 ft). *C. javanica*, the apple blossom cassia, is also fast-growing but evergreen. Its flowers, which occur in dense racemes in spring and summer, change from dark red to pale pink—a species to cherish. Cassias are generally fast growing. Although some species are quite short-lived, they grow easily and rapidly from seed. And some are quite cold-tolerant. They like light soils, good drainage and plenty of summer watering. Don't fertilise them with nitrogen, as they're legumes and produce their own. It's best to plant them in open, sunny positions, and on the whole they're easy to please. Cassias are carefree and showy. They are to warm climates what fir trees are to frigid climates—they mark the landscape.

Soft
Furnishings

With the architecture of the garden defined, the soft furnishings can follow. These are the finishing touches and can be treated like interior furnishings—choices can be made according to colour preferences, outdoor living habits, views from windows, and so on. Lush, sculptured, colourful and exuberant, these soft furnishings are a decorator's delight.

The options are many. There are flowering vines in every hue—some of which bloom all year round—that are invaluable in small gardens for filling vertical space. Shrubs include several that are really neglect-proof and many others suitable for containers. Again, the colours are strong and bright, and against evergreen foliage the effect is rich and lively.

Soft furnishings also include an exciting range of flamboyant foliage plants—aroids such as philodendrons and taros, and many species with colourful striped and speckled leaves that look suspiciously like indoor plants brought outdoors.

Then there are the accents and fillers that can light up the lower levels—cannas, gingers, and zantedeschias in bright new colours. Bromeliads, too, with their distinctive rosette forms, are decorator plants ideal for containers and confined spaces. Ferns belong in similarly moist areas, and there are many warm-climate species to grow in the shade. Other optional decorating touches include orchids, many of which need little care but flower for months on end.

Plants for dry areas are included too: brightly coloured, upright kangaroo paws, trailing ground-covers, succulents, and that design masterpiece, the wonderful spiral aloe, *Aloe polyphylla*.

And finally, there's a selection of plants for bog and water areas—species from warm climates that grow profusely, multiply easily and strengthen the impression of natural informality.

89

Climbers

Climbing vines make superb soft furnishings in the subtropical garden. Some people may wish to keep such finishing touches to a minimum; others may go all out with festoons of hanging curtains. Bear in mind that climbing vines are not just ornamentation. As well as giving maximum display for minimum ground space, they can screen out unwanted views and eyesores, provide barriers against city fumes and noise, create privacy, camouflage ugly buildings or utility areas, soften hard lines, tie buildings to landscapes, and create shade where it's needed—as well as providing flower colour or scent, or both.

Vines can be grown over posts, arches, trellises, fences, walls, pergolas, tree stumps, statues, light poles—or even in trees or over specially constructed frames. The appropriate support depends on the climbing mechanism of the particular plant, and climbers can be divided into four broad kinds: those with aerial roots/suction pads that adhere to surfaces (ivy is a good example); twiners and twisters (pandoreas); tendril climbers (passionfruit); and scandent plants, which 'throw' themselves over supports (plumbago).

Most climbing plants originated in forest clearings and margins, and along water-courses. The forest floor was cool and moist, and consisted of many layers of decomposing humus; overhead was the canopy. Close at hand were supports of varying height, from small grasses, shrubs and saplings to mature trees. The climber's purpose was to get to the uppermost canopy to the sunlight. In their natural environment, climbers didn't always end up at the top of the nearest tree; rather, they tended to take a circuitous route, looping up over one support before trying another, then perhaps back to the ground before finally ending up in a tree top many trees away. Once that canopy was reached, they would spread out to form their own mass of foliage, sometimes smothering trees in the process.

With succulents as the main exception (the climbing *Aloe ciliaris*, for example), it's a good general guide to think of climbers in terms of this forest habitat and to aim to approximate these conditions as closely as possible. The roots should be shaded from the sun, in soil that is well drained, deeply fertile and evenly moist, with generous mulching; appropriate vertical support and plenty of open sunlight at the top are also important. These conditions are especially important in the first few years after planting. Once a sound root system has developed, many climbers can tolerate limited dry spells. Whatever the support and whichever the species, all climbers grown in home gardens will need pruning—some more often than others—for home gardens are not forest wildernesses.

When it comes to selecting species, the warm-climate gardener has a great advantage over those who till cool soils, for far more climbing plants originate in tropical and subtropical climates (more than ninety per cent) than in cooler zones. With so many species of climbing plants suitable for subtropical conditions, it is difficult to make recommendations. How do you agree on beauty? About twenty years ago, an attempt was made to do just that.

Questionnaires were sent out to 100 plantsmen around the world, who at that time were considered the most experienced, travelled and knowledge-able of their kind, to see if they could reach agreement on the world's most beautiful vines. They did, and the results were published by Edwin A. Menninger in his volume *Flowering Vines of the World*. The following selection of climbers recommended for subtropical gardens includes most of those in Menninger's list.

Petrea volubilis, the sandpaper vine or queen's wreath, probably enjoyed high exposure in its original Mexican habitat, for it dislikes shade, prefer-ring day-long sun and tolerating considerable drought once established. However, it performs better if protected from wind. Growing to an ultimate height of about 6 m (20 ft), with as wide a spread, *P. volubilis* is a twining climber with narrow, rough, leathery leaves. Throughout spring and summer

Left, above: The well-known purple morning glory, *Ipomoea purpurea*, is intermingled with bougainvillea, a combination of intense colours typical of the tropics.

Left: The sun-loving *Petrea volubilis* blooms so profusely that it will smother its support in a rich mass of starry, purple flowers.

Above: Both foliage and flowers of *Distictis buccinatoria*, the Mexican blood flower, make it worth growing, especially where a screen is needed.

Previous page: Palms provide the structure in this garden, and lower-growing aroids, ferns, shrubs and ground-covers constitute the soft furnishings.

it produces arching stems with massed racemes of starry flowers, lilac with darker blue sepals. The flowers drop soon after opening and the darker sepals remain. The flowering is impressively profuse, and although it often takes several years to flower, it's worth the wait. There is also a white form, which is less readily available and less spectacular.

Distictis buccinatoria (syn. *Phaedranthus buccinatorius*), also from Mexico, needs warmth and full sun to flourish. In these conditions, it provides brilliant colour over a long flowering period. Evergreen and vigorous to the point of being rampant, it climbs by means of tendrils, has 10 cm (4 in.) leaves and 12 cm (5 in.), curved trumpet flowers in bright coral-red, flushed yellow at the base. It needs a very sturdy support and plenty of room to spread.

Among the *Solanum* species, from that large and interesting *Solanaceae* family (of which the potato, the tomato and the fruiting tamarillo are members), are a number of strong-growing climbers. *Solanum jasminoides* is the common white potato vine, a semi-evergreen, scrambling climber with small, white or bluish white flowers. Its ease of cultivation and year-round flowering have made it the petunia of climbing plants: it bedecks garages and carports, trails over trellises and fences, and can be seen clambering over every kind of post and pillar of suburban gardens. *S. seaforthianum* is evergreen, with star-shaped, lilac flowers in clusters, followed by red berries. *S. wendlandii* has bright green leaves and large, lilac-blue flowers with bright yellow centres, and can flower profusely when given a warm and sheltered spot. In cooler temperatures it flowers more lightly and is deciduous in winter.

This brilliant specimen of *Bougainvillea* 'Scarlet O'Hara' smothers both its own foliage and the fence supporting it. The flowers, actually coloured bracts, last for months on end.

S. wendlandii needs care when being handled—not for the plant's sake but the handler's. The thorn-like prickles on the undersides of the leaves are extremely sharp and can tear the skin of the unwary. *S. crispum* and *S. rantonnettii*, the blue potato tree, are both shrub-climbers, which send out long, pliable stems that can be trained up walls or fences, though they're more often found growing as shrubs. The flowers of both are deep purple with yellow centres.

The giant of the *Solanaceae* climbers, and indeed of all climbers, is the massive *Solandra maxima* (syn. *S. nitida*), the golden chalice vine or cup of gold vine. The enormous flowers (to 25 cm/10 in. long) are yellow-gold with five maroon stripes lining the inside of the chalice-shaped blooms, which have a vanilla custard scent. The equally impressive buds are twice the size of household light-bulbs. Needless to say, it needs ample accommodation. It's tolerant of sea air and can fill a large gap in a coastal garden.

Of smaller dimensions but similarly robust are the flamboyant bougainvilleas. These evergreen or semi-evergreen climbers are well suited to home gardens because they are tamable creatures that respond well to pruning, rewarding with dazzling colour. The range of cultivars includes the classic red 'Scarlet O'Hara' and the purple 'Magnifica Traillii' as well as orange, apricot, white, pink, cream and yellow, some bi-colour mutations, and some recent cultivars with striking, variegated leaves. The brilliance of bougainvilleas is actually the bracts surrounding the small and inconspicuous flowers. They're easy to grow, and revel in warmth and sun. Though they can respond to good soil and moisture by romping away over tree or house, pruning and root confinement produce the best show. Bougainvilleas are one of those climbers categorised as 'leaners'—they're excellent planted at the top of a steep slope or retaining wall and allowed to hang down. They can also be shaped as shrubs or even as standards.

Beaumontia grandiflora, the herald's trumpet, is a twining climber of Indian origin. In a sheltered site its large, shiny leaves are lush and attractive, but if exposed to wind the leaves become torn and unappealing. The white, trumpet-shaped, gardenia-scented flowers are streaked with green and are borne in clusters in spring. Beaumontias need a great deal of warmth and moisture, as well as appropriate support and space. It's also possible to train a plant to a small tree shape.

Two species of *Tecomanthe* with rampant climbing habits are *T. speciosa* and *T. venusta*. The New Zealand native *T. speciosa* was saved from extinction on the Three Kings Islands in 1946. Cuttings taken from a solitary specimen have ensured its survival, and today it is readily available. It has thick, shiny leaves, and mature plants bear clusters of waxy, cream, tubular flowers in spring. It needs shaded roots in moist soil, and the richer the soil mix the better. Juvenile vines can take quite a bit of shade just as long as there is sun waiting to be taken advantage of higher up. *T. venusta*, with flowers the colour of crushed strawberries, cream inside, comes from New Guinea. It requires a warmer growing environment than its New Zealand cousin, conditions that can be achieved with a sheltered semi-enclosure or other contrived microclimate. Like *T. speciosa*, *T. venusta* has dense foliage, with tubular flowers, hanging in clusters. *T. dendrophylla*, with deeper rose-maroon

Top: The aristocratic *Beaumontia grandiflora*—both leaves and trumpet flowers are large and stately—is a heavy vine needing strong support. The flowers are richly scented.

Above: *Tecomanthe venusta* has handsome, shiny leaves all year round but is enhanced in spring by pink, tubular flowers. It needs warmth and shelter to flower well.

flowers, also from New Guinea, is equally rare. But the pink *T. hilli*, native to Queensland, is not quite as tender as the New Guinea species and is worth growing. It has shiny leaves and trumpet-shaped, rose-pink flowers, lighter pink inside. Several exciting new tecomanthe cultivars are likely to be decorating gardens in the near future.

At the other extreme are the diminutive herbaceous climbers such as the evergreen *Asarina* (syn. *Maurandya* or *Maurandia*) species. *A. barclaiana* has purple flowers, and *A. erubescens* has pink, gloxinia-like flowers. These modest little plants could not be less demanding of space or support. They are, therefore, ideally suited to growing in very small gardens and confined patios. They grow to no more than 2–3 m (6.5–10 ft) and like plenty of sunshine. So light and gentle is their growth habit that it is possible to plant an asarina together with a larger climber and it will thread its way through the host. *A. erubescens* could be combined in this way with *Petrea volubilis* for a pink and purple mix, of *A. barclaiana* with the white *Mandevilla laxa* and any of the pandoreas.

Rhodochiton atrosanguineum is another small and dainty climber, which, like the asarinas, grows easily from seed to flowering in one season. The flowers are bell-shaped, dark red-purple (the common name is purple bells), with long, protruding, black corollas. They hang down below the foliage on thread-like stalks. *R. atrosanguineum* grows to about 3 m (10 ft) and is usually treated as an annual.

An Australian native that shares this amenable quality of being quietly unassuming and non-aggressive yet pleasantly decorative is *Sollya heterophylla*, the western Australian bluebell. It has dainty foliage and can be grown as a scandent shrub, a wall covering, or spilling from a container. Its appeal is two-fold because the bright blue flowers are followed by purple berries.

Against foliage that is unmistakably lily-like, *Bomarea multiflora* blooms in clusters of a dozen or more thin, tubular flowers with spotted throats.

Exotic in shape and colour, and irresistably eye-catching, *Gloriosa superba* 'Rothschildiana' glows in this shady recess.

Needing full sun, it rarely grows more than 3 m (10 ft) and is well suited to small gardens.

Another group of climbers that are modest in habit are the *Bomarea* species, known as climbing alstroemerias and in appearance very like this close relative. Apart from their value as cut flowers, they are very useful for filling semi-shaded sites, which they prefer, and for never becoming rampant. They need shelter, rich, moist soil with good drainage, and plenty of mulch. In response to such care, they turn on a bright display of oranges, apricots, reds and yellow-creams, all with spotting inside the tubular flowers. Although there are claimed to be as many as 120 species of *Bomarea*, a smaller number are known and grown. *B. multiflora* is probably the best known, and the most reliable and easy to grow. It grows to about 3 m (10 ft), often, though not always, dying back to ground level in winter; in summer it bears umbels of tubular, orange flowers spotted mahogany inside. As they are twining climbers, the best support for bomareas is a large mesh trellis.

Then there are the glorious gloriosas. Sprouting from winter-dormant tubers, these climbing lilies, *Gloriosa superba*, put on an impressive summer display of brilliant crimson and yellow flowers with reflexed petals. They require the same conditions as bomareas: semi-shade and cool, moist roots. Unlike bomareas, though, gloriosas have extremely fragile tuberous roots, which are easily damaged by careless planting or digging up, or—if the plant's presence is not marked during its winter dormancy—by innocent weeding and cultivating in the area. As well, the tubers are highly vulnerable to rotting in wet winter soils. In regions with heavy winter rainfalls, it's best to lift them and store them in a dark, cool, dry place until spring. The tubers can be divided every six years or so. As long as the ground has moisture and nutrition during the growing period, gloriosas will thrive in either acid or alkaline soils. The species *G. superba* has slightly smaller flowers of paler colouring than the selected form *G. superba* 'Rothschildiana'.

Sandersonia aurantiaca, occupying a perhaps doubtful classification as a climber, has urn-shaped, globose, orange flowers resembling Chinese lanterns. It is similar to the gloriosa in its winter dormancy and growth habits, and the flowers, like gloriosa and bomarea species, are excellent for cutting and floral arrangements.

Two quite different *Thunbergia* flowers on similar foliaged vines: *T. grandiflora* (top) has soft, lavender-blue flowers, while the hanging racemes of the intriguing, tubular *T. mysorensis* are burgundy and yellow.

Littonia modesta, another climbing lily similar to gloriosa, has golden yellow flowers hanging from the leaf axils and grows up to 2 m (6.5 ft) high.

Prominent in any list of warm-climate climbers are the thunbergias. All of them thrive in hot, moist conditions, and all of them, prolific in flower, bring to subtropical and warm temperate gardens an exotic, tropical touch. *Thunbergia grandiflora*, the blue trumpet vine, is probably the best known. Its pale blue-lilac flowers are a familiar sight on trellises and fences, which its lobed and toothed leaves and wiry stems entwine with tenacity. Given very warm and moist, well-drained conditions, *T. grandiflora* really takes off, so much so that in northern Queensland, along riverbanks where conditions suit it well, it has become a persistent weed. In cooler climates its growth and flowering are more restricted, and in such areas it needs protection from wind. There's also a white form, *T. grandiflora* 'Alba'. *T. gibsonii*, from East Africa, produces brilliant orange, 5 cm (2 in.) wide, flared trumpet

Trachelospermum jasminoides, a reliable climber for both full sun and semi-shade, is seen here covering a hand-rail. In spring and summer it scents the air with its fragrant, white, starry flowers. It can be grown equally well as a ground-cover.

Opposite: Two flowering passionfruit: *Passiflora caerulea* has prominent cream coronal fringes; *P. coccinea* (bottom), in brilliant red, has tall, protruding stamens. Both evergreen vines are tendril climbers.

In a warm, sheltered environment, *Stephanotis floribunda* will produce exquisitely perfumed flowers.

flowers, which, when the vine is grown in the tropics, appear for nine months of the year. In the subtropics, it's usually grown as an annual. It can tolerate a slightly drier atmosphere than *T. grandiflora*. *T. alata* has flowers of a similar colour but smaller, flatter and with a beady black centre that has given it the name black-eyed Susan. It is a widely popular climber, even being grown in cool climates as an annual, and is probably the easiest to grow of all the thunbergias. It reaches about 2.5 m (8 ft). A thunbergia of quite different appearance is *T. mysorensis*. The funnel-shaped flowers of this intriguing climber hang in 45 cm (18 in.) racemes of golden yellow and burgundy—a dramatic show. *T. mysorensis* is not as common as the other thunbergias and not as easy to propagate. It is evergreen, and in favourable conditions it reaches about 6 m (20 ft). The evergreen *T. coccinea* has smaller funnel-shaped flowers, which are scarlet-orange at the throat and have crimson lobes. These are produced in late summer and autumn. Again, the warmer and moister the conditions, the more vigorous the growth.

Scented flowers have so far been excluded from this survey of climbers—except for the beauteous *Beaumontia grandiflora* and the huge, cream flowers of *Solandra maxima*—but they should not be excluded from the garden. The subtropical world has some admirably perfumed climbers. *Mandevilla laxa* (syn. *M. suaveolens*) is a deciduous climber with summer-borne, gardenia-scented, white flowers followed by striking, long pods, with seeds that self-sow readily. *Phaseolus caracalla*, the snail flower, with fleshy, pink-lilac flowers shading to pale yellow, tightly curled and sweetly fragrant, is an easily grown evergreen plant for a sunny spot, reaching 4 m (13 ft). *Stephanotis floribunda*, that dark green, thick-leaved climber with waxy, white flowers of heady perfume beloved by florists, is a plant best grown in warm, moist, well-drained soil. *Hoya carnosa*, the well-known Australian evergreen climber, is called the wax flower for good reason—the clusters of perfumed flowers look as if they have been carved from wax in creamy white to pink shades, with ornate stars decorating the centre of each small flower. Hoyas need restrained watering and are more often grown in containers than in the ground because they need the sheltered conditions and the roots prefer confinement. *Quisqualis indica*, the hard-to-obtain Rangoon creeper, produces hanging clusters of starry, rose-pink flowers with long, slender tubes and is sweetly scented. *Trachelospermum jasminoides*, the star jasmine, can be fairly slow to start but is a robust climber that excels in covering trellises and camouflaging supports with its attractive evergreen leaves—there's a variegated form too. It also makes a superb ground-cover. Its masses of star-shaped flowers are highly fragrant, resembling citrus flowers.

Many of the scented climbers are white, cream or near white in colour. By contrast, the vibrant red- and yellow-flowered climbers are not usually scented.

Passion flowers, *Passiflora* species, are an important group of climbers, their place in the subtropical garden being akin to the place of the clematis in the cool-climate garden. The genus comprises more than 500 species, native to a dozen different countries. A passion flower is unmistakable: five sepals and five petals (together called 'tepals') around a corona made up of rings of thread-like filaments with a central column of five stamens—an artfully coloured, elegant construction. The flowers captured the imagination of the Spanish priests who were the first Europeans in South America to identify the vine and claim that it represented the crucifixion of Christ, hence its common name.

Passiflora vines are grown for both fruit and flower. The best-known species is *P. edulis*, grown for its large, round, dark purple fruit, although its flowers are as striking as any. The so-called banana passionfruit, *P. mollissima*, is a rampant, evergreen vine with pale pink flowers and 12 cm (5 in.) long, thin-skinned, golden fruits. It can reach 12 m (40 ft) and, like all passion vines, needs pruning. *P. antioquiensis* is another banana passionfruit valued for its ornamental red flowers. *P. coccinea* will stop you in your tracks with its vivid red flowers. These open to about 12 cm (5 in.) and can appear all year round but most often in winter. From tropical South America, it needs really warm growing conditions to perform well. *P. alata* has red flowers; *P. amethystina*, as the name implies, has purple-blue flowers; and *P.* x *exoniensis* is a hybrid for hot climates and has rose-pink blooms. *P. cinnabarina*, an Australian species, has wrinkled leaves and small, pendulous flowers; *P. caerulea*, a Brazilian species, has bluish mauve flowers with darker purple and cream trimmings and is highly prized. All *Passiflora* species need full sunshine, mild winters and rich soil—the richer the better.

A highly decorative group of twiners is the Australian genus *Pandorea*. *P. pandorana*, with the common name of wonga-wonga vine, climbs vigorously to 10 m (33 ft) or more and bears 3 cm (1.5 in.) long flowers that are cream coloured with maroon spotting. *P. jasminoides*, the bower vine,

Metrosideros carminea, a climber related to the New Zealand native pohutukawa, produces a brilliant display of flowers in spring.

has clusters of trumpet-shaped, white flowers with pink throats. Many attractive cultivars are now available, including the showy *P. jasminoides* 'Alba', *P. j.* 'Rosea Superba', *P. j.* 'Charisma', and *P. pandorea* 'Golden Showers'. They are evergreen, the leaves are glossy and of neat, attractive appearance, and they'll grow in full sun to light shade, though they prefer their roots to be shaded. They respond well to pruning, and they're not rampant, making them ideal for covering carports, pergolas, tree stumps, decking and so on; and they combine well with other climbers. As climbing plants, pandoreas are first-class.

Two climbers related to the pandorea are the look-alikes *Podranea ricasoliana*, the pink trumpet vine or Port St John creeper, and *Clytostoma callistegioides*, the violet trumpet vine. Both are fast-growing, evergreen vines and both have pastel, flaring trumpet flowers with darker fine lines on their throats: clytostoma's flowers are lilac and podranea's are rosy pink. Give them humus-enriched, slightly acid soil in full sun with strong supports, and feed and water them during hot months.

Another famous Australian genus, as much in garden cultivation as the pandoreas, at least in its native country, is *Kennedia* (syn. *Kennedya*). These are rampant, leguminous vines, most of which come from fairly dry parts of Australia and so can tolerate some drought. They abhor waterlogged soil—nothing kills them faster. Like their culinary pea relatives, kennedias prefer slightly alkaline soil. *K. coccinea* could claim to be the showiest of the genus, widely recognised for its profuse, scarlet, yellow-centred flowers. *K. rubicunda*, with its dull, coral-red flowers, is called the dusky coral pea. *K. nigricans*, the intriguing black coral pea, has unusual deep purple-black flowers with yellow blotches at the centre. *K. beckxiana* has pink and green flowers. Those of *K. macrophylla* are brick-red and yellow; while *K. retrorsa* is grown for its blooms in eye-catching magenta-pink.

Eustrephus latifolius, the wombat berry, is a lesser-known Australian native, gentler in habit than the kennedias, evergreen with wiry stems that twine to around 3 m (10 ft). The dainty flowers are borne in spring—hair-fringed, starry flowers in white or pale pink, about 1.5 cm (0.5 in.) across—and these are followed by bright orange berries.

Cobaea scandens, cup-and-saucer vine or cathedral bells, is an easy tendril climber for the subtropical garden, growing rapidly from seed to full flowering in its first season. The bell-shaped flowers, sitting in large calyxes like cups in saucers, open lime green and age through mauve to deep purple. The form 'Alba' has lime-green flowers that age to cream. *C. scandens* grows best in well-drained, moist soil sheltered from wind.

The genus *Metrosideros*, which includes the beautiful New Zealand native pohutukawa, has several species of attractive climbers. *M. carminea*, akakura, is the most brilliant, producing flowers in such abundance that they often conceal the small, dark green leaves. *M. albiflora*, akatea, has white flowers and large, leathery leaves; *M. fulgens*, aka, bears bright orange flowers; *M. robusta*, the rata, though spectacular in bright red bloom, grows too large for urban gardens, eventually turning into a massive, 30 m (100 ft) tree.

The genus *Ipomoea*, best known for its celebrated morning glory flowers, includes a very special flower that performs an impressive nocturnal ritual:

the moonflower. *Ipomoea bona-nox* (syn. *I. alba* and *Calanyction aculeatum*) is a frost-tender, easily grown climber, producing large, glistening, white flowers that open at night. The flowers' opening is a ritual so dramatic that admirers have been known to hold moonflower-opening parties! *I. bona-nox* will grow well in containers, as root restriction encourages flowering; and while reaching a height of 3 m (10 ft) or so, the plant is inclined to be floppy and responds well to pruning. Another member of the *Convolvulaceae* family is *Mina lobata* (previously *Ipomoea versicolor*). It shares the characteristic vigorous climbing habit, but the flowers, unlike most of the open, flaring shapes of the ipomoeas, appear as slender racemes of thin tubes, first crimson, then orange turning yellow, and finally white.

Senecio macroglossus is one of those climbers that grow so easily they can naturalise. It is one of the few climbing members of the daisy family, *Asteraceae*, and it has the double virtue of displaying fleshy, ivy-like leaves, always a fresh green, together with yellow daisy flowers, surprisingly fragrant. Native to South Africa, this twining vine is often called Cape or Natal ivy. *S. macroglossus* 'Variegatum' is a variegated-leaf form.

The next few are 'leaners' or 'throwers' that straddle the shrub and climber categories. *Bauhinia scandens* is an evergreen climber with fabulous, fragrant flowers, pale pink and orchid-like with red stamens, borne profusely over

Once established, *Podranea ricasoliana*, the pink trumpet vine or Port St John creeper, is easily grown and undemanding; given warmth and full sun, it puts forth a lively display of pink throughout summer and autumn.

the entire plant, giving it an exotic appearance evocative of the tropics. *B. galpinii*, the scarlet-flowering bauhinia, is a clambering shrub (see page 113) but can be trained up a support.

Allamanda carthartica, the golden trumpet, functions similarly as both shrub and climber. It's a strong, robust plant that needs space and warmth but will tolerate coastal conditions if watered adequately. The evergreen, glossy leaves, coupled with its ability to cover eyesores—grown at the base of a bare bank, allamanda will move up and cover it in no time—make it attractive all year round. As a wall cover, however, it tends to be rather untidy and needs tying in place. The large, yellow, funnel-shaped flowers, which bloom for a long period in summer, are very showy, and it's altogether a splendid and highly desirable climber. The cultivar 'Hendersonii' has the largest flowers and is recommended. Two other allamandas are *A. neriifolia*, the golden trumpet bush, a shrub with deeper golden flowers, and *A. violacea*, with purplish red flowers.

The flamboyant *Pyrostegia venusta*, flame flower or golden shower, is an evergreen tendril climber and a Brazilian member of the *Bignoniaceae* family. It is robust in habit, tolerating very hot through to frost-level temperatures, with dense foliage, tenacious tendrils, and profuse, flaming orange, tubular flowers in drooping panicles from autumn to spring. *P. venusta* puts on a dazzling show, and once established it's fairly drought-tolerant.

Are oranges, reds and crimsons more common in warm climates than in cool? Given the intense hues of such typically warm-climate climbers as the bougainvilleas, it would seem so. The observation has already been made that strong light intensifies these colours, whereas in higher latitudes the softer light does more justice to the pastels, which might pass unnoticed in Cairns or Cairo. At any rate *Mandevilla splendens* (syn. *Dipladenia splendens*) produces a flower that is a gloriously rich rose-red. Perfectly suited to warm and humid gardens (it's a Brazilian native), it needs good support. It's moderate and restrained in growth, so it should never need pruning. It can be grown in a container, provided the site is well ventilated, but does better in the ground in well-drained, moist soil—and mulching is essential. It prefers a moist atmosphere. In a small, subtropical garden, and when well cared for, *M. splendens* is irresistible.

There are other mandevillas: *M. sanderi* 'Rosea', the Brazilian jasmine, has large, pink flowers with yellow throats and gives a long display; *M. boliviensis* (often erroneously called *M. alba*) has yellow-throated, white flowers; and the deepest red of all, in a dark pink-crimson, comes from the cultivar *M.* 'Red Riding Hood'. *M.* x *amabilis* 'Alice Du Pont' is a popular, twining evergreen from Brazil. The impressive trumpet flowers are very large and very pink, and will bloom almost all year round if the site is sufficiently warm and sheltered.

Antigonon leptopus, or corallita, is the wonderful Mexican mountain chain (also called chain of love or coral vine), the common name referring to its hanging racemes like strings of coral-pink necklaces. It is fast-growing, evergreen and requires perfect drainage, but it is not always available. A shade more red but still described as 'coral', the globular flowers of *Berberidopsis corallina*, the coral plant, hang down on slender threads like clusters of cherries,

Handsome in both deep pink flower and glossy foliage, *Mandevilla* x *amabilis* 'Alice Du Pont' is an ideal climber for a small garden.

100

throughout summer. This is a tender, shade-preferring twiner that must have acid soil and wind protection to succeed, but it's most elegant when it does. It's evergreen, with attractive, oval, leathery leaves, and grows slowly to around 3 m (10 ft).

Redder still, or scarlet-orange, the flowers of the tropical climber *Clerodendrum splendens* are admirably light and bright in contrast to its dark green, evergreen foliage. This is a tender one from equatorial Java and needs true heat to thrive. *C. thomsoniae* is better known, most commonly as an indoor or glasshouse climber. Its flowers are red and white, and appear in dense clusters—very ornamental.

Orange-apricot flowers make a splash of colour in late summer wherever *Campsis radicans*, the trumpet vine, is grown. This well-known, deciduous vine from the southeastern United States has clusters of trumpet-shaped flowers up to 7.5 cm (3 in.) long. *C.* x *tagliabuana* 'Mme Galen', often mislabelled *C. grandiflora*, has darker, medium-sized flowers. *C. chinensis* (syn. *C. grandiflora*) has large, apricot flowers that hang down. *Canarina canariensis*, the Canary Island bell-flower, has large, hanging bells that are a true orange. This is a low-growing climber, moderate in growth, that dies back in late summer to bloom in late winter and spring. It needs a shady, protected spot.

Campsis x *tagliabuana* 'Mme Galen' is a deciduous climber that bears masses of flowers in summer and autumn.

Yellow daisy flowers (*Senecio macroglossus*) and yellow allamandas have been mentioned, but there are other yellow beauties that command attention. One is *Macfadyena unguis-cati* (syn. *Doxantha unguis-cati*), whose common name is cat's claw. Given day-long sun, wind protection and warmth, this fast-growing evergreen will respond with a display of beautiful, canary-yellow, lopsided trumpet flowers. Then there's *Hibbertia scandens*, the Guinea gold vine, from Australia. Its open, saucer-shaped flowers are more gold than yellow, and its oblong leaves are glossy and deep green. It has a useful preference for dry, sandy soils, thriving even on sand dunes, and makes a good ground-cover. *Gelsemium sempervirens* is the celebrated Caroline jasmine, native to the United States. It's an evergreen twiner but performs equally well as a 'spiller'. It also has the double blessing of a long flowering season and fragrance—not to mention the shining, yellow, trumpet-shaped flowers. *G. sempervirens* is pest-free and not rampant, happy in most situations.

If blue and purple seem under-represented among climbers, try the hardenbergias, such as *Hardenbergia violacea* (there are pink and white forms), the solanums or thunbergias described above, *Petrea volubilis*, or the sprawling shrub-climber *Plumbago auriculata*. *P. auriculata* (syn. *P. capensis*), the leadwort, is an easy-going, mild-mannered plant whose beauty lies in the soft colouring of its sky-blue, phlox-like flowers. And it definitely benefits from pruning.

One of the sunniest yellows imaginable, *Macfadyena unguis-cati* (syn. *Doxantha unguis-cati*) tumbles over its wooden support.

102

Shrubs

In the exotic garden, shrubs contribute depth, texture and colour—yet they're a dispensable option. It's perfectly possible to paint the entire picture using only bold architectural forms without a shrub in sight. However, shrubs from hot countries often flower with such colour intensity that to place them among the many greens in a lush planting is to bejewel the mantle. Lush foliage absorbs and balances bright colours that in a temperate garden might seem harsh or garish.

The shrubs included here are mostly densely foliaged and evergreen, spreading, sprawling or upright; few of them exceed 3 m (10 ft). Those discussed first have been selected because they are easy to grow and dependable; those that follow are grouped according to flower colour; and finally, two genera tailor-made for the subtropics are given individual attention.

The first of the easy-to-grow shrubs is the indestructible oleander, *Nerium oleander*, that ubiquitous bush with flowers in pink, white, red or apricot for many months of the year. Oleanders tolerate poor soil, air pollution, coastal sand—valuable virtues offset by the fact that the whole plant is poisonous to people and animals, and that even burning prunings will emit toxic fumes. *N. oleander* is fast growing to 3 m (10 ft) and more, with as wide a spread, but can be trimmed to any size.

The Australian native bottlebrush, *Callistemon viminalis*, offers similar neglect-proof qualities. Acacias, also Australian natives, grow as both small trees and shrubs, and there are a few that are quite drought-tolerant, such as *Acacia conferta*, *A. suaveolens* (sweet-scented wattle), *A. subulata*, *A. drummondii*, which, unlike most acacias, prefers shade, *A. pulchella*, and the very low-growing, wide-spreading *A. cultriformis* (knife-leaf wattle).

A softer-stemmed bush from Africa, which revels in dry sun, has the alliterative name of *Leonotis leonurus*. The orange flowers are borne in whorls on tall stalks in summer and autumn. It's an easy plant to grow (to 2 m/6.5 ft) and is improved by grooming. The popular *Lantana camara*, unmatched for providing bright splashes of colour—in shades of reds and yellows, oranges and pinks—can be sited just about anywhere and is not fussy about soil.

Though *Cestrum* species like moisture and humidity, they are otherwise very undemanding. They have a tendency to rank growth and ragged leaves, and therefore need pruning—but how deliciously they scent the night air. Night jasmine or queen of the night, *Cestrum nocturnum*, is one of several common names alluding to this potent perfume. *C. diurnum*, the day jessamine, is similar, with cream flowers of unexciting appearance; *C. aurantiacum* has bright orange flowers in summer and smells of crushed mandarin skins; *C. fasciculatum* has purple-red flowers; and *C. parqui*, so easy to grow that it borders on invasive, has cream flowers but still with that heady night scent. While the other species need plenty of water, *C. parqui* can survive droughts. All are fast growing (to around 2.5 m/8 ft) and respond well to pruning.

In bright rusty orange, the flower whorls of *Leonotis leonura* are said to resemble lions' tails. It's an ideal shrub for sunny, dry spots.

Leptospermum cultivars, with aromatic foliage and effusive flower sprays in spring, are ideal shrubs for beginner gardeners or for those with no time to spare. While the New Zealand native species *L. scoparium*, or manuka, can top 4 m (13 ft) in the wild, the newer cultivars are smaller and more compact, with names such as 'Keatleyi' (pale pink), 'Nicholsii' (crimson), 'Snow Flurry' (white), and the more prostrate 'Wairere', with red-veined, white flowers. *L. scoparium* var. *rotundifolium* has particularly large, pink flowers. Leptospermums will grow almost anywhere.

Both *Solanum laciniatum*, the New Zealand native poroporo, and *S. rantonnettii*, the blue potato bush, are very good for filling gaps, and can be left to their own devices or disciplined with shears. They need warmth and moisture but little else to produce their deep purple flowers with bright yellow centres—small but profuse.

Abutilons, or Chinese lanterns (*Abutilon* x *hybridum* cultivars), have the same requirements. These rather sparsely structured, evergreen bushes have nodding bells almost year round—in white, orange, pink, yellow or red—and will grow in sun or shade. *A. megapotamicum* has smaller, yellow and red, bell-shaped flowers. Abutilons respond well to pruning.

The business of recommending 'easy' plants is hindered by the knowledge that what may be a happy discovery for one gardener may be an accursed weed to another. Just as *Cestrum parqui*, for example, or the ginger plant, *Hedychium gardnerianum*, have gone wild in northern New Zealand, so this next recommendation, which grows tamely in New Zealand, has become a noxious weed in northern Queensland.

Ochna serrulata, the Mickey Mouse bush, is a fast-growing evergreen (to 2 m/6.5 ft) that prefers an acid soil but is tolerant of wet or dry conditions, wind, salt air, sun or shade. Its buttercup-yellow flowers are followed by residual sepals, which turn bright scarlet and surround shining black berries in their centres (hence the common name), all of which is very ornamental. Be warned: it is lavishly self-seeding.

The intriguing, bright red sepals follow the yellow flowers of the Mickey Mouse bush, *Ochna serrulata*.

When well grown and in full flower, *Brunfelsia latifolia* becomes a mass of colour in many shades of purple-blue. Grow it in sheltered shade.

Now for flowering shrubs grouped according to colour. With the possible exception of the soft, powder-blue of *Plumbago auriculata*, none of these blues are true blue—deep purple-blue, mauve-blue and lavender would be more accurate descriptions.

The floriferous brunfelsias surprise by producing blooms in all of these shades and even some in between. The flowers, purple when newborn, gradually fade until they become white, and a bush will have flowers at different stages of fading at any one time, hence the common name of yesterday, today and tomorrow. When well grown, the glossy-leaved, evergreen and fragrant-flowered shrubs are ravishing. They require warmth, shelter from wind (by all means grow them on a patio or in a container—they seem to flower well with restricted roots), fertile soil and, above all, shade from hot sun and copious amounts of water in summer. *Brunfelsia latifolia* is the most fragrant species, while *B. pauciflora* 'Macrantha' has the largest flowers.

Iochroma cyaneum, like the brunfelsias a member of the *Solanaceae* family, has deep violet flowers that hang in clusters of long, narrow tubular blooms among the large and somewhat limp and felty leaves. It is evergreen and needs a warm spot in full sun with moist soil. Though the flower colour is intense, the overall appeal is lost if this 3 m (10 ft) bush is not well trimmed.

Eupatorium sordidum has mauve puffball flowers resembling the perennial ageratum. With large, crinkly leaves and red stalks, it grows to about 1.5 m (5 ft) high with an even wider spread, producing its fragrant flowers in spring. It, too, is best grown in moist, well-drained soil in partial shade.

The flowers of *Iochroma cyaneum* hang in bunches of eye-catching violet. The insides of the tubular blooms are often a lighter shade.

105

The sumptuous colours of tibouchinas are far from delicate—they enliven the late summer and autumn garden with bold, intense colour. Top: *Tibouchina urvilleana*. Above: *T. granulosa*.

Thunbergias are known mostly for their climbers, such as the popular *Thunbergia grandiflora*, but *T. erecta* is a creeping, sprawling, evergreen shrub. It has small, oval leaves, densely arranged, and produces flaring, tubular, violet flowers, yellow inside the tube, in summer. It rarely exceeds 1 m (3 ft) in height, though it can spread widely. *T. erecta* comes from tropical Africa and needs hot, moist conditions to do well.

Mackaya bella is a glossy-leaved shrub with pale lavender flowers traced with veins of dark maroon. It seems best suited to warm, if not hot, sites in half-shade, under taller trees, where it likes to have its roots in leaf mould. A showy shrub, *M. bella* is slow growing to about 1.5 m (5 ft) and rarely needs pruning. It needs plenty of water in summer.

By contrast, *Duranta repens* is fast growing and tolerant of drier and more exposed conditions. Its violet-blue flowers (one of its common names is sky flower) are small but profuse all summer. Golden berries (another of its common names is golden dewdrop) follow the flowers and hang from drooping branches in winter. There is also a variegated form as well as a white-flowering version. An evergreen shrub, *D. repens* is loose and willowy in habit, and can exceed 3 m (10 ft) if not trimmed.

Plumbago auriculata, with powder-blue flowers, is a semi-climbing shrub up to 3 m (10 ft). It can be pruned as either a shrub or a climber. Left to its own devices—and given the room—it is loosely spreading, fairly open in foliage, and flowers through summer and autumn. It needs full sun and benefits from moisture in summer.

Tibouchinas (syn. *Lasiandra*) are right at home in exotic gardens—their flower colours are dazzling and vibrant. From South America, they are known for their evergreen, velvety leaves and intensely coloured flowers, such as the purple species *Tibouchina urvilleana* or the mauve-pink *T. granulosa*. New forms are becoming available, some with even larger purple flowers and others in lilacs and pinks. Prone to wind damage, they grow and flower best if pruned immediately after flowering (heights of species vary from about 2 to 5 m/6.5 to 16.5 ft or more) and groomed. They need full sun in good soil, with additional moisture during dry periods.

Alyogyne huegelii is the so-called blue hibiscus. (Though it is a member of the same family, neither this nor any hibiscus is blue.) It is a fast-growing, upright to rounded, evergreen shrub, to about 2 m (6.5 ft), with coarse, toothed leaves. The flowers are lavender, with overlapping petals, often described as being like the blades of a ship's propeller. Native to western Australia, it likes a warm, dry climate, and hence is widely grown in California. It doesn't require extra watering, but it does need protection from wind if it is to look its best.

Ruellia macrantha is another of those tropicals with brilliantly vivid flowers. It's a fast-growing but short-lived shrub that produces its quilted, violet-pink flowers in late autumn and winter. *R. macrantha* needs a warm, sheltered site shaded from full sun in summer.

There are two oddly tall plants in the purple-lilac category that look as though they belong closer to the ground with their perennial peers but instead have bolted upwards. The giant-leaved, violet-flowering *Wigandia caracasana*, which reaches 3 m (10 ft) but can be pruned, is evergreen and

Ruellia macrantha is a fast-growing but short-lived shrub that produces its brilliant flowers in late autumn and winter.

produces its flower-spikes in spring. It has a tendency to sucker. The tree dahlia, *Dahlia imperialis*, with its plate-sized, pale orchid-pink flowers with yellow centres atop arched woody stalks, flowers in autumn before dying back to the ground. There is also a white form available. Both shrubs bring exotic flair to any garden, and both are easily grown in a warm climate.

The last of the purple-blue-flowering shrubs, though bluer than most, is very variable in performance. Sometimes *Clerodendrum ugandense* will deck itself in summer with lively blue flowers suggestive of its common name, blue butterfly bush, but sometimes the display is disappointing. It does best in a warm, sheltered position with good moisture in summer.

Among yellow-flowering shrubs, the sunny cassias must come first. (For tree species, see page 86.) *Cassia alata*, the deciduous candle bush, grows to about 2.5 m (8 ft), its golden yellow lantern spikes held aloft, as the name implies. *C. fruticosa*, the drooping cassia, is scandent, to 4 m (13 ft), and bears pale yellow flowers. *C. renigera* is deciduous and its flowers are pinkish yellow. *C. laevigata*, a tall shrub, puts on a profuse display of vivid yellow. *C. didymobotrya*, from tropical Africa, the golden wand or popcorn bush, needs a sunny, hot spot to produce flowers almost year round, though, as with most cassias, the heaviest flowering is in spring and summer. The cup-shaped, golden yellow flowers open out of shiny, blackish brown buds in summer and autumn. *C. eremophila* is a smaller shrub with a bluish tinge to its foliage, while *C. bicapsularis*, bearing large golden cups, grows and flowers so energetically that it has become a weed in subtropical America. *C. corymbosa* is probably the easiest species to grow (though cassias on the whole are easy) provided it has full sun. Two species that will tolerate a very dry climate are both native to Australia's semi-desert: *C. artemisioides*, silver cassia, with narrow, silver-grey leaves and glowing, sulphur-yellow blooms, and *C. nemophila*, desert cassia, a very similar species in flower, in size (2.5 m/8 ft), and in drought- and cold-tolerance. They're a lively bunch—and they're but a few of the several hundred cassia species native to all subtropical areas of both hemispheres. As legumes, their foliage has those distinguishing, small,

The purple-flowering *Wigandia caracasana* has huge leaves, which contribute to its tropical appearance.

pinnate leaves; their flowers all have fine petals and protruding stamens and are followed by long pea pods, which hang until they fall.

Thevetia thevetioides is a shrub with unexpectedly yellow flowers—unexpected because this shrub is similar and related to oleanders, which are always pink or red, and because this yellow is so intense. Evergreen, with thin, dark green leaves, *T. thevetioides*, like the oleander, is poisonous in all its parts. Aside from that, it's a brilliant flowering plant. The trumpet flowers occur from winter to the end of summer. It is fairly drought-tolerant and, without pruning, can reach 4 m (13 ft). *T. peruviana*, the be still tree, is hardier but less spectacular.

This next one is very special. By one of those extraordinary quirks of nature, a chance seedling from the Australian native frangipani—a tree that can reach a tall 10 m (33 ft)—developed permanently dwarf characteristics. Still with the soft golden flowers and powerful fragrance, this dwarf *Hymenosporum flavum* is a cushion-shaped bush and never exceeds 1 m (3 ft). It is also tolerant of poor soil. While its commercial life has only just begun, this is certainly a shrub to seek out in the future.

Pachystachys lutea, the lollipop plant or golden candles, is so-called because of its cheerful spikes of golden bracts surrounding small, white flowers, which shoot up from evergreen foliage each spring. *P. lutea* makes a bright display to a little over 1 m (3 ft) and prefers half-shade.

Caesalpinia gilliesii has clear yellow flowers with long, red threads (stamens) arching outwards like some exotic plumage—hence the common name, bird of paradise shrub. Because it's inclined to be straggly, and because the flowers are so lively, this species can be grown to best (and neatest) effect on the sunny side of a house wall. It reaches 3 m (10 ft) in height but double that in spread. *C. pulcherrima*, the dwarf poinciana, has cup-shaped flowers in a gaudy orange. This species grows erect, slightly taller but not as wide as *C. gilliesii*, and shares its fern-like leaves. Both shrubs need full sun and well-drained but moisture-retentive soils, are tolerant of coastal conditions, and, when established, are drought-tolerant. Caesalpinias have the drawback of being short-lived. They need to be grown from seed and don't transplant easily.

Orange is not a common colour among shrubs, since most oranges incline towards scarlet. *Mitraria coccinea* is a useful little shrub—or semi-climber—with decorative, tubular, orange-red flowers in spring. It prefers moist, acid soil in shade or half-shade and a moist atmosphere. The flowers of *Burchellia bubalina* (wild pomegranate) are also on the reddish side of orange. A relation of the gardenia, sharing the latter's glossy, evergreen foliage and sweet fragrance, *B. bubalina* develops into a dense, mounded shrub about 3 m (10 ft) high and almost as wide. It flowers for a long period. Native to South Africa, it needs well-drained and well-enriched soil, and half-shade to full sun.

Drejerella guttata (syn. *Beloperone guttata*) is the memorable, burnt-orange-flowered shrimp plant. The overlapping bracts are deep salmon at the base and taper to a pale creamy salmon in a bi-colour arrangement and in a shape that is indeed shrimp-like. *D. guttata* needs full sun and reasonable soil, is tolerant of some drought, and grows to about 1 m (3 ft).

There is one orange-flowered shrub that is so thoroughly and utterly

Top: The upright flower-spikes of *Cassia alata*, the candle bush, contrast with the horizontally held foliage.

Above: *Burchellia bubalina* offers dense foliage and bright orange-red flowers in spherical clusters.

Above, right: No brighter orange is to be found than in the profuse flowers of *Streptosolen jamesonii*, the marmalade bush.

orange that it hits you in the eye. *Streptosolen jamesonii*, the marmalade bush, has small, oval, crinkled leaves, usually evergreen, soft herbaceous stems, and bright orange, bell-shaped flowers in clusters. It prefers sun and good moisture, and grows to about 1 m (3 ft) high and as much wide.

Many white-flowering shrubs are scented. It's one of the interesting ploys of nature that if flowers cannot lure their pollinators by colour, they'll do it with smell, which is why white flowers so often smell sweet. *Murraya paniculata* could well have the sweetest flower of all, but its other attributes are equally commendable—in fact, it could be grown for its leaves alone. These are small and neat (almost 6 cm/2.5 in. long), glossy green, and densely borne, making it useful for screening and even hedging. The strong fragrance of the clusters of small, white flowers is rich and citrusy. In really hot climates the shrub will flower on and off all year round; otherwise it's a summer and autumn flowerer. Though fairly slow growing, it will reach an ultimate height of 3 m (10 ft) with a similar spread. To get there, and to produce its beautiful flowers in abundance, it needs copious watering and mulching. Pruning, though it's not really needed, will induce heavier flowering.

Luculia grandifolia has huge, oval leaves, red-veined and rather brittle, and enormous flower-heads. A big, robust, evergreen bush, which rapidly reaches 3 m (10 ft), its scented flowers—among the most fragrant of all—are actually composed of a mass of individual tubular flowers. It likes hot sun but cool roots, as its large leaves would indicate. Heavy pruning after flowering is essential.

Gardenias need no introduction. The evergreen leaves are glossy and the flowers are famous. Long associated with tropical gardens, with romance, with Tahitian legends, and with a fragrance beloved by florists as well as toiletry manufacturers, the gardenia is the one shrub to grow if you want scent above all else. But it must be grown well. Gardenias have big appetites

for moisture, especially in the air, for fertile soil, calcium (bone dust, not lime), lashings of mulch or mulch-peat mixes, and a pretty high acidity level. They also need part-shade and are less likely to thrive in full sun. There are dwarf species such as *Gardenia augusta* 'Radicans' and several medium-sized ones, while the largest is the tall-growing (to 3 m/10 ft) *G. thunbergia*.

So closely related to gardenias that it was once included in the genus, *Rothmannia globosa* has similar but larger leaves, a taller, more tree-like growing habit, a recognisable gardenia scent, and similar sustenance requirements. But the resemblance stops there, because the flowers of *R. globosa* are flaring cream bells. It can reach 3 m (10 ft), and in Australia it has been grown as a hedge.

The coffee bush, *Coffea arabica*, is strongly recommended for the subtropical garden because it's a beautiful, compact shrub with glossy, green leaves and fragrant, white flowers. It needs warm, moist air, semi-shade in its early years, a good, rich soil with as much compost as you can give it, and regular watering. Given these conditions, it can be both a landscaping and a culinary asset. It will set fruit, and the berries, when red, yield two beans each. The beans can be roasted, and yes, you can drink the brew, but you'll need a lot of berries to start filling storage jars!

Another fragrant, fruiting shrub is the Natal plum, *Carissa grandiflora*, which grows as a vigorous thicket or hedge in its native South Africa. It has treacherous thorns but brings much pleasure with its fragrant, white flowers. Natal plums prefer a drier climate than the humid subtropics, but in conditions to its liking, especially coastal, it bears delicious, red, strawberry-like fruit with red flesh and white juice.

Bouvardia longiflora is a soft-stemmed, evergreen, spreading, small shrub, reaching 1 m (3 ft) high at most but inclined to be straggly. It needs plenty of moisture, and prefers moist but drained soil. The flowers, borne in late summer and autumn, are white, slender tubes, sweetly scented.

Brugmansia, formerly *Datura*, with its massive, hanging trumpets, belongs

Left: The Natal plum, *Carissa grandiflora*, has scented, white flowers and edible fruits.

Right: While the leaves of *Luculia grandifolia* are large and rough to the touch, the scented, white flowers are captivating. Plant it in a warm spot by the house to make the most of the fragrance.

110

in exotic gardens. Aside from the flowers, the shrub is ungainly, producing spreading branches from a woody trunk, and has a top-heavy canopy (usually to 3 m/10 ft). The felty, often chewed leaves are not particularly appealing, but those bewitching trumpets are. The largest of them reach 30 cm (12 in.) in length, and the petal ends taper into recurved points. Plants need fertile, well-drained soil in a sunny position but sheltered from wind, and should be given extra water in dry periods. They revel in heat, take most of spring and summer to get going, then perform endlessly through late summer and autumn, scenting the night air for miles around.

Of some thirty or more species, *B. suaveolens*, white angel's trumpet, is

The peach–pink trumpet flowers of this *Brugmansia* look exotic and decorative in a lush setting. Their rich perfume is an added attraction.

The fragrant, white flowers and red calyxes of *Clerodendrum trichotomum* are followed by blue berries.

one of the best known and most fragrant, along with *B.* x *candida*, which has semi-double and double flowers. *B. arborea* has smaller flowers. The coloured species are less common. *B. chlorantha* is yellow, *B. sanguinea* has yellow and orange-red flowers, and there are also species and a number of cultivars in shades of yellow, apricot, peach and salmon.

A shrub or small tree with a preference for acid soil and moisture is *Gordonia axillaris*. This species looks like, and is related to, camellias, with camellia-like, dark green leaves. Its flowers are the size of saucers and have bright white petals and yellow stamens. Cold-tolerant and relatively easy to grow, *G. axillaris* can reach 4 m (13 ft).

Montanoas produce masses of white daisy flowers with yellow centres throughout autumn and winter. Both *Montanoa bipinnatifida*, the Mexican tree daisy, and *M. hibiscifolia*, from Central America, are evergreen, with large tropical-looking leaves on branching stems, which are best pruned at the end of flowering. They can reach 2.5 m (8 ft).

Clerodendrum philippinum is a compact, evergreen to semi-deciduous shrub (2.5 m/8 ft), fairly undemanding provided it has plenty of moisture, with pleasing, pinkish white, fragrant, double flowers in summer. *C. trichotomum* is much hardier, even frost-tolerant, and its fragrant, white flowers leave behind red calyxes, which in turn produce bright blue berries. It has a tendency to sucker. Both shrubs have large, fairly coarse leaves typical of all clerodendrums.

And so to red- and crimson-flowered shrubs: *Odontonema strictum* has lively red flower-spikes and shiny leaves, and grows easily. It looks par-

Right: Two species of moonflower: the shrubby *Datura meteloides* and the climbing *Ipomoea bona-nox*.

112

ticularly dramatic in a lush garden surrounded by large-leaved plants such as aroids, where its fairly small flowers are shown to advantage, and where the larger-leaved species will protect it from wind damage. It likes moist, well-drained soil and full sun or half-shade, and responds well to pruning.

On close inspection, the red of the flowers of *Cantua buxifolia* is a shimmering mix of pink and purple, yellow and orange, with an end result of rich rose-red. *C. buxifolia* comes from the Andes and has the common name of sacred flower of the Incas. Apart from its beautiful, tubular, pendent flowers, it's worth growing for its small, evergreen leaves and soft, twiggy stems, which grow to a rounded bush about 1.5 m (5 ft) wide and high. It likes full sun and humus-rich, well-drained soil. It can tolerate some cold, and once established is quite drought-resistant. A less well-known species with orange flowers is *C. tomentosa*.

Malvaviscus arboreus (2 m/6.5 ft), a species belonging to the same family as the hibiscus genus, has soft, serrated, bright green leaves and brilliant red flowers with closed-up petals from which protrude long hibiscus stamens. *Greyia sutherlandii* (2.5 m/8 ft), the mountain bottlebrush, from South Africa, has serrated, leathery leaves and spikes of bottlebrush-like flowers in bright orange-red. It likes drier conditions and a fast-draining soil, and does well in pots. *Clianthus puniceus* (1.5 m/5 ft), the New Zealand native kaka beak or parrot beak, grows into a rambling, spreading shrub with ferny leaves and drooping clusters of bright red, claw-like flowers in spring. The fiery red clerodendrums—*Clerodendrum speciosissimum, C. paniculatum* and *C. splendens*—though rampant in their low-altitude, equatorial homes, are a bit on the tender side in a subtropical garden and need winter protection. Another brilliant red, a small plant that literally drips with scarlet pendants in late winter, comes from high altitudes and can take some cold. *Agapetes serpens* is a little gem. To encourage it to bedeck itself with its electric Christmas lights, give it acid soil, sharp drainage and semi-shade. The red flowers of *Iochroma coccineum* hang in clusters of thin tubes like those of its sister species, the purple-blue-flowering *Iochroma cyaneum* (page 105); and it has the same growing requirements. *Erythrina* x *bidwillii* has bright red flowers in early summer.

Euphorbia pulcherrima, that familiar winter-flowering poinsettia, grown indoors and out, needs fast-draining soil and full sun to produce its blazing crimson bracts. *E. milii*, the crown of thorns, is a wickedly spiky, semi-succulent shrub with bright scarlet bracts enclosing small, yellow flowers; and another euphorbia, *E. fulgens*, the most tender of the three, has small flower bracts in vivid orange-scarlet.

Bauhinia galpinii, the pride of de Kaap, is a sprawling, clambering shrub whose elegant, orchid-like blooms are bright brick-red. *B. galpinii* grows to about 3 m (10 ft) and, while needing space to spread, is easily pruned.

Two red-flowering shrubs are especially recommended: *Calliandra* and *Metrosideros*. Both genera are well suited to subtropical gardens, being easy to grow in containers and in the ground, and both give a lot for little effort. Their flowers are made up of dense stamens—calliandra means 'beautiful stamens'. Calliandra's pinnate leaves are light and fern-like, and the flowers are described by the common name powderpuff bush. *Calliandra tweedii*

Erythrina x *bidwillii* is a shrubby species in this genus of coral trees.

113

Opposite: *Hibiscus rosa-sinensis*, a symbol of the tropics, has a long flowering period, and many cultivars have been produced in a wide range of colours.

Opposite, below: Hibiscuses can look especially effective in mass plantings of different cultivars. They go well with dramatic foliage plants such as palms and silver-leaved astelias.

Calliandra's common name of powderpuff bush is apt. In spring and summer it is smothered in fluffy-stamened flowers.

The dense foliage and tolerance of coastal conditions, along with its brilliant scarlet flowers, make *Metrosideros collina* 'Tahiti' a very desirable shrub.

(1.5 m/5 ft) is the most cold-tolerant species and is commonly grown. It bears its crimson blooms throughout spring and summer. *C. haematocephala* is a slightly larger bush with pink-stamened flowers, while those of *C. surinamensis* are rose-pink, and those of *C. portoricensis* are fluffy white. All calliandras do well in reasonable soil in full sun.

As for the *Metrosideros* shrubs, these sparkling species native to Pacific Islands, with cultivar names like 'Hawaiian Fire', flower freely almost year round. *M. collina* 'Tahiti' is a deservedly popular small bush that grows to around 1.5 metres (5 ft), with cheerful, bright, fiery scarlet or orange-scarlet blooms. And there's also the dwarf shrub form (to 90 cm/36 in. high) of the robust forest climber *M. carminea* (see page 98). This was a chance discovery when *M. carminea* was being propagated by cuttings.

The flowers of *Dais cotinifolia* are exceptionally ornate. They're like pale pink, spherical heads of laced fretwork, the shape of which has led to the common name of pompon tree in its native South Africa. It is sometimes likened to the cool-climate daphne because of its fragrance—both are members of the *Thymelaeaceae* family. Easily grown in an open, sunny position, *D. cotinifolia* is a large shrub or tree and requires a fast-draining soil. It can be encouraged to grow multiple trunks and become shrub-like, or pruned to a single-trunked, slender tree when young. Although its ultimate height can be as much as 6 m (20 ft), it makes a good garden specimen when kept under 3 m (10 ft).

Rondeletia amoena is an evergreen suitable for sun or shade, with the attraction of honey-sweet flowers. Its dense flower-heads, made up of tiny, pink, yellow and salmon tubes, also appeal to bees. *R. amoena* grows to about 2.5 m (8 ft), with glossy leaves and a neat appearance.

There are two groups of shrubs, not yet touched upon, that are tailor-made for the subtropics, flowering spectacularly. The first is that flamboyant siren of sea coasts and islands, the hibiscus. The genus *Hibiscus* actually comprises more than 200 species. Far from being limited to the Pacific Islands, they're scattered around tropical, subtropical and some temperate regions, on forest edges, mountains, even deserts and mangrove swamps. *Hibiscus rosa-sinensis* is the most favoured species in cultivation and has given rise to hundreds of successful cultivars. These are tough, tolerant of salt air, reasonably easy to grow and attractively foliaged for most or all of the year; the flowering period is long and the blooms are lavish. The colours are manifold: pure white through ivory and beige to cream, yellow, gold and numerous different shades of pink and red. There are two-colour combinations with contrasting centres and stamens, petal frills in lighter or darker hues—and more.

This wealth of colour, together with its preference for growing alone rather than in the company of other plants, makes the hibiscus the logical choice for people who want open spaces or lawn, with only an occasional

The flowers of the new hybrid 'Southern Belle' strains of hibiscus have huge, flat petals, seen here in a mix of pinks.

tree or shrub, but double-duty colour. It's ideal for seasiders who'd really rather be off on a boat. In a fuller garden, though, a backdrop of dense, lush foliage allows hibiscus flowers to glow like jewels. Some of the more outstanding cultivars, including recent award-winners as well as enduring classics, are: 'Summer Samba' (sizzling yellow-red), 'Celia' (frilly apricot), 'Old Frankie' (lush cyclamen-pink), 'Madonna' (white with a red centre), 'Firedance' (red fire), 'Isobel Beard' (lilac—the nearest to blue—with a red eye), 'Gay Nineties' (tri-coloured blooms of yellow, ivory and rose-pink centre), 'Halekala' (rich yellow), 'Vasco' (bright lime-yellow with a white centre), 'Ruby Brown' (as close to brown as any flower can get), 'Thelma Bennell' (one of the brightest hot purple-pinks imaginable), 'Cameo Queen' (an award-winning luminous lemon), 'Kinchen's Yellow' (bright yellow and very floriferous), and 'Mary Wallace' (winner of many awards and exceptionally decorative in hot tropical red etched with gold). In New Zealand the range known as the 'Jack Clark Hybrids' have achieved deserved fame for their high-quality flowers.

H. rosa-sinensis requires good-quality soils and plenty of moisture. The pH level should be neutral to slightly acid. It needs potassium (but not derived from muriate of potash) and trace elements in the kind of mix available in citrus fertilisers. These fertilisers should be applied in spring and early summer—never in winter—and only to maturing plants, since a newly planted hibiscus in a good soil has no need of additional feeding.

While *H. rosa-sinensis* holds the lead for proven garden performance, there are other species that have their own charm and should not be overlooked. *H. syriacus*, the Syrian rose, is deciduous and grows to about 4 m (13 ft). Its bell-shaped flowers range in colour from white through mauve-blue to violet and red, and include some of the bluest, such as the cultivar 'Ardens' or the deeper violet 'Blue Bird'. While *H. syriacus* is better suited to cooler gardens than subtropical ones, although withstanding hot, dry summers, it is worth growing for its range of pastel colours.

H. arnottianus is native to Hawaii and little known outside those islands, although the species has been-crossed with *H. rosa-sinensis*. It deserves to be more widely available. Not only do the small but delicate white flowers with red stamens last for two days (other hibiscus flowers last one day only), but they are distinctly fragrant. In addition, *H. arnottianus* is a long-lived, evergreen shrub resistant to root rot and borer. *H. schizopetalus* has the appearance of a rare exotic. The single flowers hang down, their extraordinarily long staminal column suspended below, contributing to the unusual effect. 'Schizopetalus' means split petals, the streaky pink and red petals being more feathery than those of other species. An evergreen or semi-deciduous shrub, it's definitely a warm-climate species, intolerant of cold and poorly drained soil.

H. moscheutos is best known as the parent of some recent and very popular hybrids, the giant-flowering 'Southern Belle' strains, which were preceded by the almost-as-large 'Dixie Belle'. Both strains come in white and shades of pink and red, with deeper-coloured centres. These hybrids have enjoyed enormous commercial success—and justifiably, considering that they're frost-tolerant, heat-tolerant, compact (to 1.8 m/6 ft), can be grown from seed, flower the first season, and bear blooms up to 30 cm (12 in.) in diameter. For hibiscus lovers, they're a dream come true. They can be grown as bedding plants and are effective in massed plantings. Note, though, that 'Southern Belle' hybrids need a bit more care than other hibiscuses, being more easily damaged by wind and insects, and it's usually necessary to stake them.

H. tiliaceus, the hau tree of Hawaii, is an evergreen, salt-tolerant tree, attaining a mature height of 5–6 m (16.5–20 ft) but prunable to a smaller size. It grows best in moist soil with full sun, bearing its flowers intermittently throughout the year but prolifically in summer.

Another group of shrubs that grow superbly in the subtropics and have stunning flowers are vireya rhododendrons. When hybridists got hold of these so-called 'tropical rhododendrons' they had a field-day. The crosses and mixes and matches of colour, shape and scent resulted in some rare triumphs.

Behold the vireya. It's a plant for all seasons and a shrub with every attribute. It's evergreen, compact, easily grown, prunable, untouched by slugs and snails, rarely affected by disease, has handsome foliage, is perfectly suited

Three vibrant vireyas provide colour in this lush setting: the yellow-throated, pink 'Kisses', orange 'Golden Charm' and 'Pink Delight'.

to subtropical climates, and bears trusses of showy flowers that are good in vases and often sweetly scented. Although a few bear but once or twice a year, many flower intermittently throughout the year. The colours range from pure white to sizzling magenta, with plenty of creams and pastels, bi-coloured blooms, and several sumptuous beauties with lightly shaded petals etched with darker margins.

Most reference books and plant catalogues lump vireyas together with temperate rhododendrons as though they're all much the same—they're not. Almost all vireyas are epiphytes, and that's a crucial difference, especially when it comes to growing them. As epiphytes, they don't grow in the ground but grow naturally on stumps, tree forks, rocks, rotting logs or similar footholds, where they are nourished by forest debris and frequent rainfalls. Vireyas come from forest habitats in New Guinea, the Malay archipelago, the Philippines, Borneo, Indonesia, and one species from the far north of Australia. Although these countries are equatorial, altitude modifies an otherwise tropical climate. The conditions in their natural habitat include high humidity, high UV light, and frequent, swirling cloud and rain showers followed by bright sun. Those species that come from highest up grow well in gardens with coolish temperatures (even tolerating a hint of frost); the greatest number of species, which come from mid-altitudes, enjoy mild climates; while those that come from near sea level like it really hot.

Where strong doses of UV light are combined with warmth and humidity, conditions for vireyas are ideal. Success comes from remembering their epiphytic origins: they need air around their roots, so should be planted on the soil, not in it. The plant should be positioned in a shallow depression and the roots covered with a good mix of fine bark and compost (they prefer a slightly acid soil). Plants should be staked for the first year or so until they have anchored themselves, with mulch applied at intervals. In other words, replicate as far as possible the conditions of their origins. Although they'll need watering for their first few seasons, vireyas are more drought-tolerant than temperate rhododendrons. It's a sure bet that gardeners whose vireyas have languished, wilted or worse have not grown them in this way but planted them deep in an airless hole. Waterlogged roots are fatal.

The species found growing in the wild vary greatly, from spindly shrubs with narrow leaves and thimble-size blooms to towering, large-leaved shrubs with big, breathtaking flowers. *Rhododendron leucogigas*, has lavish flower-heads composed of about ten individual funnels the size of a cupped hand, in pearly white edged with deep pink margins, long-lasting when cut and exquisitely scented. Though reluctant to bloom ouside its native New Guinea, its size and scent are features of its hybrid offspring. Other notable species, all now used extensively in parenting wondrous progeny, include *R. christianae* (bright yellow shading to orange); *R. jasminiflorum* (small flowers, white flushed pink and highly disease-resistant); *R. javanicum* (orange-red with rose throat and stamens); *R. konori* (very round leaves, large, rather lax, white flowers, scented); *R. laetum* (a brilliant yellow flower—a classic—and much used in hybridising); *R. lochae* (red, the only native species from northern-most Australia); *R. loranthiflorum* (a small-leaved, sweetly scented, white-flowering species); *R. orbiculare* (blush-pink, scented, and good for hanging baskets); *R. superbum* (so large that mature bushes become terrestrial in their native habitat, with massive, creamy white flower-heads, heavily scented—but proving infuriatingly resistant to growing in cultivation); *R. zoelleri* (a stunning bright orange-red); *R. tuba* (medium-sized, white, tubular flowers); *R. macgregoriae* (light bright yellow); *R. commonae* (small flowers, in both a red and a cream form); and *R. christi* (curved, tubular flowers in bright red).

The task of attempting to choose the best of the vireya hybrids, while ignoring others, is not easy. However, agreement is likely on some of the following: 'Cameo Spice' (superb large, scented flowers in honey-apricot shades); 'Buttermaid' (pale, clear yellow); 'Silken Shimmer' (pink and gorgeously perfumed—one of the best scents of all); 'Java Light' (glowing orange); 'Gilded Sunrise' (rich yellow-apricot); 'Pendance' (small flowers, pale pink); 'Pink Delight' (an 1860 hybrid, pink, and very frequently in flower); 'Rob's Favourite' (vermillion); 'Kisses' (yellowish centre opening to light pink); 'Tiffany Rose' (deep rose-pink); 'Carillon Bells' (cyclamen-pink); 'Ne Plus Ultra' (bright, bright red and one of the fullest flower trusses); 'Lulu' (butter-yellow throat opening to apricot); 'Golden Charms' (rich apricot); 'First Light' (pale pink); 'Coral Flare' (deep coral-pink and almost continuously in flower); 'Hot Gossip' (rich claret); 'Princess Alexandra' (small, white flowers flushed pink, lightly scented); 'Lipstick' (white flowers edged with pink margins); and one of the most floriferous of all, 'Dawn Chorus' (pale apricot flowers with cream-yellow centres).

Vireyas are exciting shrubs to grow. Their natural preference for restricted roots means that the gardener can be inventive in selecting sites for them—even trying them as epiphytes. Against the foliage of other plants, where the backdrop is dense and dark, vireyas make a colour splash like no other.

Flamboyant Foliage

While large-foliage plants can define the garden's framework, smaller-growing plants with dramatic and colourful foliage can fill the spaces below. Shield-shaped leaves are characteristic of many of these species; so, too, are long stalks, leaves with contrasting ribs and etched veins, shiny surfaces and intricate patterns. All of them are eye-catching.

Aroids (members of the *Araceae* family) are sculptured and lush in appearance, and are dynamic plants for the subtropical garden. Until recently, aroids haven't featured very much in home gardens, being more common in rainforests or tropical taro plantations. However, they are being used increasingly by landscapers in warm climates for their strong visual impact. The *Araceae* include over 100 genera and more than 2,500 species. Their distinguishing feature is the flower or inflorescence, which consists of a fleshy spadix surrounded by a large, petal-like spathe or bract, often very showy. This distinctive flower is most easily recognisable in the common arum or calla lily, *Zantedeschia aethiopica*. The other distinguishing feature of aroids is the way in which new leaves emerge—from the base of another leaf, under the protection of a cataphyll or sheath. After the new leaf has emerged, the cataphyll dries out and fades, sometimes becoming papery or turning brown.

Many aroid species grow on forest floors in areas of high humidity; a few are known to have adapted to living on dry rock faces, some in cool, open regions; and some are true bog plants. Aroids need warmth and lots of moisture to do well, and they prefer shade to sun. Their variety and form invite creative landscape use: Roberto Burle Marx, noted for his restrained use of plant diversity, designed a garden in Brazil using only rocks, water, and a felicitous selection of aroids. Some of the most commonly recognised aroids are house plants—monsteras, philodendrons, anthuriums, dieffenbachias, aglaonemas and spathiphyllums, for example. These exotic rainforest inhabitants grow easily enough in containers indoors but, with some exceptions, seldom produce flowers.

Monstera deliciosa, the Swiss cheese plant or fruit salad plant, will not flower indoors but will when grown outside. After the thick, cream-coloured spathe withers, the spadix grows larger and ripens into an edible fruit, the flavour of which is compared to fruit salad, something like a pineapple-banana mix, tangy but sweet. Although now one of the most universally popular indoor plants, *M. deliciosa* is not common in the wild—in fact, all the propagated plants in the world come from one wild specimen. The most remarkable feature of monsteras, a feature shared with philodendrons, is the holes and cutouts in the leaves, known as fenestration. These holes, which vary greatly in size, shape and number, have long intrigued botanists. It has been suggested

Right, above: *Alocasia odora*, or giant taro, showing the ribbed undersides of broad leaves. The spathe and spadix inflorescence is typical of aroids.

Right: *Alocasia* x *amazonica*, with its waved edges and ribs dramatically outlined in white, has one of the most striking leaves of any plant.

that they allow more rain to penetrate to the roots than a complete leaf, or perhaps reduce tearing by wind, or assist cooling by allowing air to circulate around the leaf. Monsteras add drama to any garden. Give them ample space, solid support such as a stone wall, and adequate moisture. They prefer well-drained, humus-rich soil. Although they prefer light to full shade, they can take full sun for their upper storey, which with steady deliberation will climb to a height of around 7 m (23 ft). Slashed, split and holed, mature leaves can reach 80 cm long and 70 cm wide (32 x 28 in.).

Philodendrons, too, have handsome architectural foliage, and almost the full range of aroid leaf shapes appear in this genus. There are many species, including evergreen shrubs and climbers. The climbing species germinate in the soil, climb trees (philodendron means tree-loving) and, keeping their base roots in the ground, develop both clasping roots to climb with as well as long feeder roots to sustain themselves. Eventually the ground roots often die off and the plants become epiphytic. Their growth habit is therefore loose and sprawling, and well adapted to harmoniously co-existing with other plants in a subtropical garden. Like monsteras, philodendrons often explore

Above: *Philodendron scandens* uses aerial roots to climb. New leaves have an attractive copper tinge.

Right: A dense ground-cover is formed by a mass planting of *Philodendron* 'Xanadu'. The red-foliaged bush to the left is *Iresine lindenii*.

The sprawling aroid *Philodendron bipinnatifidum* combines well with a young *Phoenix canariensis*.

the area around them, sending out long, slender, leafless shoots. Some species also sport holes and slashes in their leathery leaves.

There are many philodendrons. Like other indoor plants, they've taken a circuitous route from rainforest to coffee table and thence to the garden in the hope they'd adapt—and many have. *Philodendron scandens*, with small, heart-shaped leaves, and *P. erubescens*, with dark green leaves with maroon undersides and purple stalks, are both well-known climbers that, confined by containers or trimming, can be kept to shrub-like proportions. The popular indoor plant *P. bipinnatifidum* is outstanding in the subtropical garden. Given favourable conditions—shaded warmth and moisture—it produces huge, lobed and wavy blades 1 m (3 ft) in length, standing on stalks as long again, so that the whole plant can measure 2 m (6.5 ft) in height on a trunk 10 cm (4 in.) in diameter—an impressive sight. *P. variifolium* and *P. sagittifolium* also make good subjects, and there are many cultivars, such as 'Red Princess', 'Red Duchess', 'Royal Queen', 'Emerald Duke' and 'Emerald King', and some eye-catching, upright-leaved rosette forms derived from the 'bird's nest' species, *P. wendlandii*. The supreme philodendron, irresistibly sumptuous, is surely *P. melanochrysum*: the long leaves (a full 60 cm/24 in.) in deep olive-green shimmering with copper, veins etched in ivory and with margins to match, make it a compelling sight. Grow it if you can—it's fully tropical and needs heat and high humidity, but it's a prize of a plant.

Raphidophora decursiva resembles philodendrons in leaf and habit, being both a climber and a sprawling shrub in the garden. Instead of holes or slashes, though, it has evenly divided leaf segments, which differentiate it from other aroids, giving it leaves like palm fronds.

124

This lush mixed planting includes the aroid *Xanthosoma sagittifolium*, behind which is the colourful *Cordyline terminalis*, or ti. On the far right is a pawpaw (*Carica*) and on the left a small species of banana (*Musa*).

Alocasias are fellow aroids whose large leaves on long stalks display high-lighted veins, which hybridising has exaggerated. The best-known cultivars have come from *Alocasia sanderana*, which has glossy, dark green, deeply lobed leaves with striking silver veins and margins and a Y-shaped midrib. Its hybrid offspring *A.* x *amazonica* is an aroid classic. For an exotic look, it's unrivalled. Its very dark green, purple-backed leaves have silver veins and margins but are less deeply lobed than *A. sanderana*. Less spectacular but reliable in cooler temperatures is *A. cucullata*, Chinese taro. It has long-lived leaves, deep green with prominent veins, and forms an attractive, com-pact plant. Alocasias range in colour from rich purple, purple-red, a deep, almost black purple, to lime-green, olive-green, brown, blue-grey with silver veins (*A. thibautiana*), ivory, and some with banded green and white stalks with brown mottling (*A. zebrina*). *A. odora*, commonly known as spoon lily or giant taro, makes a superb garden subject. It has handsome, 1.2 m (4 ft) leaves, with prominent veins and wavy margins, on 1 m (3 ft) stalks. It is distinctive because the leaves point upwards, unlike those of colocasias and xanthosomas, which point downwards. Its cream-yellow-green flowers are highly perfumed.

Colocasias are close relatives of alocasias. *Colocasia esculenta*, taro, is believed to be the oldest cultivated crop in the world, predating even rice. Though principally a root crop, the leaves are also eaten, as are the stalks and even the inflorescences. Culinary value aside, this species offers the landscape gardener an easily grown and easily increased foliage plant, which reaches 1 m (3 ft) or more in height, with huge, fresh green leaves that are handsome all year round. The leaves are held almost vertically on long stalks. *C. esculenta* is very variable, and numerous local varieties have been identified with minor differences in growth habit, leaf shape and colour, and the size and shape of corms. Several cultivars are available commercially, including 'Fontanesia', which has green leaves with darker veins and margins and blackish leaf-stalks, and 'Illustris', with purple-spotted leaves. A form commonly known as black taro has pointed leaves with wavy margins, and dark purple-black veins, margins and stalks. Taros, like many of the aroids, are best in mass plantings. They prefer moist soil, well-drained or boggy, rich in humus, and respond well to feeding during the growing season.

Swamp taro, *Cyrtosperma merkusii*, reaches 3 m (10 ft) or more and has huge, upward-pointing blades with large basal lobes—a commanding plant in any garden.

Xanthosomas are very similar in appearance to colocasias and caladiums. *Xanthosoma sagittifolium*, tannia or cocoyam, is an important food crop but is also a decorative garden plant. It's generally larger than taro, up to 2 m (6.5 ft), but the leaves are more arrow-shaped, with the long stalk attached at the leaf margin, not part-way along the midrib like taro leaves. This is

Xanthosoma sagittifolium is thriving in rich, moist soil. To the right is a dark-leaved colocasia.

a variable species, and a number of forms have previously been given specific status. *X. lindenii* (sometimes classified as *Caladium lindenii*) comes in a wonderfully variegated form, 'Magnificum', with cream-veined, deep green leaves. It looks superb in mass plantings. Xanthosomas like similar conditions to colocasias—humus-rich soil, moisture and warmth.

There are other aroids with strong shapes. The genus *Aglaonema* includes the striking *A. rotundum*, with round, glossy, green leaves with red undersides and midribs, and the plain green *A. modestum* or Chinese evergreen. All have glossy leaves, some marbled or splotched, and while they cannot compete with massive alocasias or colocasias for size or impact, aglaonemas make excellent ground-covers in shaded spots, though they must be kept moist.

Dieffenbachias, which resemble aglaonemas but are distinguished by their South American origins, are good for landscaping as they tolerate more light than most aroids. They do, however, need partial shade and shelter, and will not stand wind. Dieffenbachias are outstanding as foliage plants. If they are given the warm, still conditions they like, with constant atmospheric humidity, their patterned foliage can illuminate the garden. There are many species and varieties, with a range of colours and markings in greens, whites and creams. Cultivars such as 'Tropic Snow', 'Exotica' and 'Wilson's Delight' are particularly handsome. A word of warning about dieffenbachias: the common name of dumb cane has sinister origins—so toxic are the leaves that even the slightest chewing or sucking of them will cause swelling of the tongue and mouth, making speech and nutrition impossible; larger quantities will have graver results.

Spathiphyllums are aroids that enjoy moist, humus-rich soil and partial shade. They have thin, elliptic leaves and white spathes and spadices. The most celebrated of these—at least the most widely marketed—is *Spathiphyllum wallisii*, the leaves of which have impressed veins and are slightly wavy at the margins. The inflorescence is fragrant. Not rampant, of modest dimensions, and able to flower indoors, its best-seller attributes were assured when it was given the common name of peace lily.

Other aroids occasionally found in subtropical gardens include caladiums, which look best mass planted as a ground-cover. Wonderfully coloured though they are, these could be just a touch too tender to remain in the ground over winter in many gardens. The best advice would be to dig up the underground tubers when the foliage has died down and let them rest indoors over winter, then replant them outside again in the spring. Even in the wild, caladiums do not keep their colourful leaves all year round, becoming dormant for several weeks or months during dry spells. Even if kept warm and damp, it appears that dormancy is part of their natural cycle, so the luminous colours of caladium leaves are likely to remain restricted to summer display. Species and hybrids include *Caladium bicolor* (green-edged pink), *C. humboldtii* (low growing, small, green with pink splotches), *C.* x *hortulanum* 'Candidum' (translucent silver with green veins) and *C.* x *hortulanum* 'Pink Beauty' (pink-mottled green).

Aroids don't always feature conspicuously in garden centres but can often be found among indoor plants.

The leaves of *Dieffenbachia* 'Tropic Snow' appear as if painted, the white and cream markings splashed on glossy green edges and midribs.

A mature bird's nest fern, *Asplenium nidus*, can be as startling as it is unmistakable. Such lush growth comes from shelter, warmth, feeding and ample moisture.

This intensive planting of foliage species includes a large-leaved *Ficus lyrata*, or fiddle-leaf fig, several varieties of croton (*Codiaeum variegatum*), *Schefflera arboricola* (left back) and *Beaucarnea recurvata*.

A remarkable fern with luxuriant foliage is *Asplenium nidus*, the bird's nest fern. In nature it is an epiphyte that grows in the forks of trees as well as in the ground, but it will also grow well in a pot, provided it has good drainage, regular watering and sufficient humidity. Care and attention (including protection from snails and slugs) will be rewarded with a stunning rosette of shining, spreading fronds up to 90 cm (36 in.) long and fresh as daybreak. *A. nidus* tolerates low light but not wind or draughts, and drought is fatal.

Back on the ground, and keeping a low profile at around 30–60 cm, (12–24 in.), are more striking foliage plants. Some of them look suspiciously like indoor plants turned outdoors—and they are. Many of those foliage plants with zebra stripes or purple blotches, speckles or colourful margins, marketed as house plants, can, in fact, be grown outside in the subtropics. They won't all survive—a lot depends on careful siting and experimenting. Here are four guidelines to help these plants to succeed: first, slug and snail bait, otherwise your newly planted treasures could vanish overnight; second, shade, not sun—if they've been growing inside they won't have had to cope with anything like the fierce midday sun of summer; third, they'll need warmth—it may even be best to acclimatise them gradually over their first cool season so that they can cope with the next—and the site should be as warm and sheltered from wind as possible; fourth, slug and snail bait. If you think the writer can't count, the writer can and has—counted dozens of criss-crossing silvery trails over the empty spot where stood, twenty-four hours before, a fresh, unblemished fittonia.

Exotics that can be tried outside—always speculatively—include: *Peperomia obtusifolia* 'Variegata' (a bushy plant to 30 cm/12 in., with round, fleshy leaves with bright green and yellow splotches) and *P. marmorata*, or silver heart (low growing, with oval, heart-shaped leaves in dull green, quilted with silver); *Sansevieria trifasciata* 'Hahnii' (a relation of the sword-pointed mother-in-law's tongue but with much wider leaves banded in dark and light green) and the yellow-edged 'Golden Hahnii'; *Pilea nummulariifolia*, or creeping Charlie (a mat-forming creeper with small, round, pale green leaves, highly textured), and *P. cadierei*, the well-known aluminium plant (with oval leaves quilted with silver); *Iresine herbstii* 'Aureo-reticulata' (a bushy foliage plant to 60 cm/24 in., with cheerful cream- and yellow-veined leaves) and *I. lindenii*, or bloodleaf (dark red leaves); *Pellionia daveauana* (syn. *P. repens*) (a ground-hugging creeper with striking colour patterns, sometimes called the water-melon begonia); *Fittonia verschaffeltii* var. *argyroneura*, the silver net-leaf plant (whose white veins imposed over olive-green leaves are embroidered perfection); and *Hemigraphis repanda* (with toothed margins on long, lance-shaped leaves with purple undersides, to 20 cm/8 in.).

Crotons, *Codiaeum variegatum*, those well-known indoor plants with leathery leaves in red, yellow, pink and orange, need a very warm spot to do well outside, for they are really fully tropical. Hybridising has produced a range of leaf shapes with contrasting, wavy margins, from as wide as 12 cm (5 in) to the narrow ribbon leaf of *C. variegatum* 'Interruption'. All need moist, rich soil in half to full shade. They have a maximum height and spread of about 60 cm (24 in).

Top: Recent hybridising of *Cordyline terminalis* has intensified the crimson colouring to produce spectacular foliage such as 'Red Sister'.

Above: *Dracaena* cultivars are available in a range of startling colour combinations, with striped leaves and contrasting margins and midribs.

This mixture of striking foliage plants includes the cream and pink-striped *Cordyline terminalis* (centre), *Sanchezia nobilis* (right) and an almost black *Cordyline* from New Guinea (foreground).

Then there are the *Marantaceae*. Like those species listed above, marantas are tropical rainforest plants requiring full shade, warmth and high humidity. They are conspicuous foliage plants. *Maranta leuconeura*, the prayer plant, is one of the best known, with wide leaves, strikingly patterned. *M. leuconeura* 'Erythroneura', the herringbone plant, has leaves in two shades of green, with cream and red veins, and is exceptionally ornate. In the same family are *Calathea makoyana*, the peacock plant, again with highly patterned foliage; *C.* x *ornata* 'Roseo-lineata', with large leaves, glossy with rib highlighting; and the very popular zebra plant, *C. zebrina*, growing to a robust 80 cm (32 in.) and holding upright its velvety, striped leaves. *Ctenanthe oppenheimiana*, the never-never plant, has long, lance-shaped, green and silver leaves undercoloured with purple. *C. lubbersiana* has leaves variegated with yellow and with yellowish green undersides. *Stromanthe amabilis*, with its richly patterned foliage, and *S. sanguinea*, with scarlet bracts, are both rather tender, tropical members of the maranta family and need temperatures no lower than 10°C, but they grow well in pots and so may be moved in times of cold. Their foliage is glossy, widely spear-shaped, and richly hued. They grow in clumps to about 1.5 m (5 ft) high.

Opposite, above: Foliage plants superbly positioned among river stones include ferns, young palms, crotons and a bromeliad.

Opposite: This undergrowth planting includes clumps of a glossy-foliaged *Ctenanthe* species as well as a young palm, ferns and bromeliads.

130

As many of these plants have tender temperaments and success is not assured, how about considering—by contrast—a plant that's so easy you can scratch a hole in the ground, drop it in, and turn your back on it? As long as there's a spot of moisture about and a bit of shade, *Chlorophytum comosum* 'Vittatum' never needs a second glance. When you come back a year later, you'll find eight or nine of these spider plants, all doing very nicely. Chlorophytums are almost abuse-proof. They have water-storage chambers in their roots and withstand drought.

Aspidistras, on the other hand, need water as well as protection from slugs and snails if they are to look really healthy. *Aspidistra elatior* is the famous cast-iron plant of Victorian drawing-rooms, able to tolerate low light and air pollution. It's not tropical; nor is it more than marginally subtropical. It comes from Japan and is a cold-tolerant, slow-growing, clumping plant with shiny, pointed leaves, very dark green, which can eventually reach 70 cm (28 in.) in length. There's also a cream-striped form, 'Variegata'.

Opposite: A young specimen of *Caryota ochlandra*, the Chinese fishtail palm, is underplanted with a mixture of foliage and flowering plants.

A robust croton, *Codiaeum variegatum*, shows the green leaves of new growth mixed with lighter and darker apricot shades, the leaves darkening with age.

The low-growing, purple-backed *Stromanthe sanguinea* needs warm temperatures, part-shade and moist soil.

133

Aphelandras are doubly ornamental plants, as their zebra-striped leaves and their cheerful yellow or orange flowers testify. Although usually an indoor plant in need of warmth and moisture, *Aphelandra squarrosa*, the zebra plant, can be grown outside, provided it's kept dry in winter and out of direct sunlight in summer.

Foliage begonias—the rhizomatous species—share with caladiums multi-coloured, shield-shaped leaves in bright pinks and lilacs. Unlike the tuberous, flowering kinds, these begonias need constant subtropical temperatures and are ideal foliage plants for gardens where the soil is rich, moist and well drained. Rex begonias are the best-known hybrids. Growing to around 1 m (3 ft) or more, their slightly hairy, highly coloured leaves (the flowers are insignificant) combine well with other ground-covers. Although they need shade, patches of sunlight during the day can illuminate the rich colours wonderfully. For a luxurious ground-cover, the rich green, velvet-leaved *Begonia floccifera*, from tropical India, is worth seeking out.

The leaves of *Coleus blumei* hybrids are similarly multi-coloured. Long popular as indoor plants, easy to grow in full or half-shade, coleuses need no description. Their serrated edges etched in cream or green and contrasting with centres of pink, claret, lilac or cerise are familiar among house plants. Coleuses need indirect light and well-drained, moist soil. To keep them at their best, straggly leaves and flower-spikes, which are insignificant, should be removed.

The burgundy-pinks of these foliage begonias contrast effectively with the tree fern fence behind and the lighter green ferns and ground-cover.

134

Accents and Fillers

Together with foliage plants, which offer interest in both shape and colour, robust perennial plants can fill gaps and provide seasonal splashes of colour to enhance the subtropical garden. Many of these warm-climate perennials tend to be bigger, bolder and more luxuriant in foliage than their cool-climate counterparts. Bear in mind that most perennials, particularly bulbs and tuberous and rhizomatous plants, are best planted in multiples, not singly. As clumps increase, they can be divided so that at flowering time the colour is replicated again and again, giving unity to the garden. Undivided clumps, especially in warm, moist environments, can soon start to occupy a lot of territory, so plan accordingly.

One group of classic flowering perennials of the tropics is the gingers. The genera *Alpinia*, *Zingiber* and *Hedychium* include more than 100 species renowned for their clump-forming habit, their fleshy leaves and their scented flowers. Although most of the *Zingiber* species (including *Z. officinale*, the plant grown for its commercial crop of ginger spice) grow only in really hot, moist, equatorial areas, a number of other species are quite subtropical. The two most prized species for the subtropics are probably the seductively

The maroon-backed leaves and richly coloured flowers of *Hedychium greenii* make it an attractive plant for growing in moist ground.

Alpinia zerumbet, shell ginger, is a tall plant with imposing foliage.

fragrant white ginger or butterfly lily, *Hedychium coronarium*, with its gleaming flowers of white satin, and *Alpinia zerumbet*, the famous shell ginger (syn. *A. speciosa* and *A. nutans*), with its ivory racemes opening to yellow and pink flowers. *A. malacensis* is similar to *A. zerumbet* but the flower-spikes are erect. *H. greenii*, the scarlet ginger, has green leaves with maroon undersides and spectacular, orange-scarlet flowers. It reproduces by means of adventitious plantlets instead of seed and requires shade and moisture to succeed. Other decorative gingers, all easily grown in mild, moist climates, include *H. coccineum*, the red or scarlet ginger, which has dense spikes of orange-red flowers with pink stamens. Like the more crimson *A. purpurata*, it brings a vivid splash of colour to the garden. The cold-tolerant *H. densiflorum* has short-lived, orange flower-spikes in summer. *H. gardnerianum*, the kahil ginger, has large gold and yellow flowers, richly scented. This species should be planted with caution because it can become invasive, as it has, lamentably, in New Zealand's native forests. One species rarely seen in home gardens but deserving of attention is the tropical crepe or Malay ginger, *Costus speciosus*. The flowers are white or pale mauve surrounded by a reddish bract—very crepey and very appealing.

Other members of the *Zingiberaceae* include *Kaempferia galidgesii*, with pink, four-petalled flowers; *Renealmia cernua*, sometimes classified as an alpinia and bearing flowers that are small and pale with orange bracts; and *Tapeinochilus ananassae*, with dense spikes of bright red bracts. All of these gingers revel in high humidity and will grow to 1–2 m (3–6.5 ft). They like light shade to full sun and deep, rich soil.

Blue ginger or Brazilian ginger, *Dichorisandra thyrsiflora*, is a member of the *Commelinaceae* family. Its erect, purple flower-spikes, unscented, arise from clumps of glossy leaves, which grow on their stems in spirals. Like the Asian gingers, this species flowers in late summer and autumn, and grows to around 1 m (3 ft). All gingers, both true and blue, can be effectively sited under overhanging foliage and at the base of large trees, provided there is adequate moisture.

136

Heliconias are large-leaved exotics with vibrant 'lobster-claw' flowers. Actually, the flower itself is tiny and it's the enclosing bracts that make the colourful display. Choosing which of these stunningly ornate species to grow is like choosing among the crown jewels. For the subtropical gardener, growing heliconias successfully will depend entirely on how tropical the conditions can be made, since heliconias are true tropical plants. This is not to say they can't be grown in the subtropics; it's just that getting them to thrive cannot be guaranteed. *Heliconia rostrata* has perhaps the merest edge on the others. Its common name is hanging lobster claws, which doesn't really do justice to the vibrant alternating bracts in scarlet-pink with tips dipped in creamy-yellow paint. It is simply sumptuous. But so are the others: *H. humilis* has sharper points tipped with green; *H. caribaea* comes in yellow, a purple variegation and a brilliant red; *H. revoluta* is bird-like in scarlet and cream; and *H. pendula* is longer and pendulous, as the name implies. *H. wagneriana* has bracts of soft green and apricot. *H. aurantiaca* and *H. psittacorum* are smaller and good for mass planting. All species reach a height of 1–2 m (3–6.5 ft), with a spread of about 1 m (3 ft).

The unfussy canna lily is bold, brazen and sizzling with tropical colour, and can be an impressive addition to the subtropical garden. The foliage of these erect, 1 m (3 ft) tall sirens is dramatic: pointed, with prominent midribs, banana-like, in green, bronze or variegated. A most striking variegated cultivar is *Canna* x *generalis* 'Striatus'. There are several species

Left: Blue ginger, *Dichorisandra thyrsiflora*, is striking in flower.

Right: *Heliconia* species are striking accents but require a tropical microclimate to succeed in the subtropics.

Cannas, popular and unfussy, come in a range of flower and foliage colours.

Clivia miniata is an ideal filler under trees, preferring full shade to maintain its dark green foliage.

of canna, such as the deep rose-flowering, 3 m (10 ft) tall *C. iridiflora*, or Indian shot, and many hybrids. In recent years breeders have concentrated on selecting larger flowers on small plants—and the blooms come in every shade, excluding blues, with many bi-colours, two-tones and spotted arrangements, as well as plain white (a recent cultivar) and plain cream. The contrast of a pale flower with deep plum-coloured foliage is among the canna's specialities. Cannas need well-mulched, deep, humus-rich soil, plenty of moisture, protection from wind, and full or almost full sun. Well-grown cannas will produce a rewarding display. Potted specimens will only grow well in deep containers.

Clivias, also shade-loving, prefer a much drier soil. The very deep green colour and clumping shape (to 50 cm/20 in.) of clivia's strap-like leaves make them ideal ground-covers and fillers under trees all year round. The orange-red flowers of *Clivia miniata* appear in winter and spring, while *C. gardenii*, which has narrower, green-tipped flowers, is autumn flowering. Cultivars with wonderful rich flower colours, fuller trumpets and heavier clusters have been raised, and more are likely to appear in future.

Arthropodium cirratum, the renga-renga lily, is also drought-tolerant and even easier to grow. Not technically a lily, being fibrous rooted, it shares the lily's clump-forming, spring-blooming characteristics, producing branched panicles of starry, off-white flowers on wiry stems. It reaches 90 cm (36 in.) and has the virtue of growing readily just about anywhere. To look its best, though, it should be grown in semi-shade to full shade, and it benefits from grooming and snail control.

Arums and zantedeschias are both aroids—those plants that feature so prominently in creating a lush and exotic effect—and are tailor-made for subtropical gardens. Though the name arum is loosely used to describe the characteristic spathe-spadix inflorescence, true arums are in fact a very small Mediterranean genus. They have arrowhead leaves, and the white *Arum italicum* has a cream-green spathe and yellow spadix. The spathe of *A. palaestinum*, the so-called black calla, is green outside and purple inside, with a black spadix. Arums can take full sun but look their best in half-shade with moist but well-drained soil. Their Mediterranean origins make them quite hardy to cold winters. *Zantedeschia aethiopica* is a white-flowering species that grows so prolifically it has become naturalised in some warmer parts of New Zealand. *Z. aethiopica* 'Green Goddess' produces large, cream-green spathes, which live up to the name. *Z. elliottiana* is the popular golden arum lily. The deep green, heart-shaped leaves have speckled markings and the spathes are a bright yellow. A spotted species, *Z. albomaculata*, with pale lemon spathes, and the pink-spathed *Z. rehmannii* are two of the lesser-known species. *Z. rehmannii* 'Violacea' has deep violet-purple spathes. What is of importance to the subtropical gardener is that hybridists have mixed and matched

The renga-renga lily, *Arthropodium cirratum*, planted underneath a Queensland umbrella tree, *Schefflera actinophylla*, and alongside clumps of young *Strelitzia reginae*.

Scadoxus multiflorus subsp. *katherinae*, with umbels of star-like flowers.

the best features of several species, aiming for smaller plants, smaller inflorescences, interesting spotted and variegated leaves, and a wide colour range. The resulting calla lilies are small, slender plants (up to 60 cm/24 in.) in red, pink, orange, purple-red and cream (sometimes collectively referred to as 'New Zealand Mixed Hybrids'). Their potential as cut flowers and for landscaping is great. As long as they have moisture, zantedeschias will grow easily in sun or shade, though they prefer shade. They are tolerant of cold, although this induces winter dormancy. Many tolerate waterlogged soil and can be grown on pond edges.

The *Amaryllidaceae* are strongly represented in the tropics and subtropics, and crinums are classics. Their enormous bulbs and lush foliage betray their origins—tropical Asia and Africa—though a few species come from the drier regions of South Africa and one from the arid Middle East. They like warmth and moisture without demanding high humidity and, in fact, usually flower better where autumns are dry. The genus is large, with many species and cultivars at home in cold regions (especially *Crinum moorei* and *C.* x *powellii*), but the recommended species for subtropical gardens are: *C. asiaticum*, which reaches 60 cm (24 in.), with thin, strap-like leaves and fragrant, white flowers with narrow, pointed petals; the more shade-tolerant swamp lily, *C. pedunculatum* (to 60 cm/24 in.), with grey-green leaves and scented flowers; the Florida crinum, *C. americanum*, which grows also to 60 cm (24 in.), with fragrant, white flowers; and, if you can obtain it, the Ceylon crinum, *C. zeylanicum*, white with red stripes, and *C. procerum* var. *splendens*, whose massive bulb produces red flowers opening to pale pink in a rounded umbel.

South Africa's blood lily, *Haemanthus coccineus*, is unlike any other—the thick stems, which grow almost leafless from the ground, to 30 cm (12 in.), are topped with dramatic red bowls densely filled with brush-like stamens. *Scadoxus multiflorus* subsp. *katherinae* (syn. *Haemanthus katherinae*), grows into a much larger clump (to 1 m/3 ft) and bears masses of scarlet, star-like flowers

Hybrids of *Hippeastrum*, or Barbados lily, come in a range of bold, hot colours.

Opposite, above: A clump of crinums and an edging of white impatiens contribute to this effective border.

Opposite: *Eucomis pole-evansii*, the largest species in this genus, needs full sun and is drought-resistant.

in umbels. The spectacular hybrids of *Hippeastrum*, or Barbados lily, come in a selection of shades from flaming red through orange and salmon-pink to white. They need gravelly, fast-draining soil in semi-shade, and grow to around 40 cm (16 in.). All of these *Amaryllidaceae* species are easily grown in pots—which may be preferred by gardeners weary of battling with snails!

Two white-flowering bulbs, one perfectly suited to the subtropics and the other requiring more warmth and a bit of coddling, are *Polianthes tuberosa* and *Eucharis grandiflora* (syn. *E. amazonica*). *P. tuberosa*, the late-summer-blooming tuberose, has funnel-shaped, single, white flowers with a rich and exotic perfume. It is justifiably valued by florists for both its scent and its vase life. These 60 cm (24 in.), erect-growing plants are very easy to cultivate provided you know how: once the bulb has flowered, it dies, leaving small offsets. The largest offsets should be selected and planted anew, and these will flower the following year. *P. tuberosa* 'The Pearl', the more common form, has double, pink-tipped flowers. Plant the tuberose in a strategic place—near seating or a social area—and enjoy one of the plant world's most intoxicating perfumes. *Eucharis grandiflora* is a tropical plant from Columbia and likes high humidity, a warm to hot temperature, fertile but fast-draining soil, and—here's the tricky bit—a lack of water in winter, to induce flowering in summer. Although *E. grandiflora* will grow perfectly well without the dry period, it is drought that triggers flowering, so if watering can be controlled, three or four flowerings a year can be induced. Fortunately, it takes well to container culture—unlike *Polianthes tuberosa*—and will grow to 50 cm (20 in.), producing lightly scented, open flowers with trumpet centres.

The genus *Eucomis*, or pineapple lily, is often bypassed by gardeners who find their arching flower-spikes and limp leaves somewhat floppy and untidy, particularly at the end of flowering, and are not won over by the sweet honey scent and the long life (about a month) of the cut flowers. These undesirable characteristics may be found in some species (*E. comosa*, *E. autumnalis*, *E. zambesiaca*), but they do not apply to *E. pole-evansii*, the giant of the genus. This striking plant grows to over 1 m (3 ft), holding its cylindrical, creamy pinkish green flower-heads proudly on strong, vertical stems—an ideal structural plant for the exotic garden. As with all of the dozen or so species that come from Africa, *E. pole-evansii* is drought-resistant and grows well in pots. In the ground plants are best left for years to increase on their own. They need full sun.

At the top of any list of flowering, low-growing plants that are easy to care for must surely come the ubiquitous impatiens, or busy Lizzie. As long as they have warmth and moisture, impatiens are fool-proof. They spread quickly, reseed easily, and will cover pots, baskets, walls, or areas of the garden. The bright colours have a tropical intensity—colours like rich magenta, shimmering cerise and hot orange—and the flowering goes on and

This variegated impatiens makes an effective mass planting in association with dramatic foliage plants such as *Schefflera* species and palms.

143

on, month in and month out. Busy Lizzies prefer half-shade rather than sun, and good soil will produce improved flowers and foliage. These bright colours look their best against dark backdrops, and plants look better if they are groomed.

Dizzying colours come also from the flowers of *Heterocentron elegans*, Spanish shawl, the rapid-spreading and useful ground-cover with intense cerise flowers; from two related trailing plant of the tropics, *Columnea* x *banksii* and *Aeschynanthus pulcher*, both known as lipstick plant because of their flower shape and red colour; and from the oranges, reds, burgundies and yellows of mimulus, that lively little, soft-stemmed plant that needs soil on the wetter side of moist to thrive.

Kohleria erianthus has eye-catching, foxglove-like, tubular flowers the colour of fire, and the same colour is repeated in the saw-tooth edging of the velvety leaves. This was one of the species used by hybridists to create the much showier modern gloxinia.

The jewel of the subtropical accents and fillers must surely be *Streptocarpus*. In the right conditions—in the wild they live on forest edges in moist, drained leaf mould, protected from wind, heavy rain and hot sun—the gorgeous flowers of streptocarpus hybrids, in blues and lavenders, pinks, mauves and

The juxtaposition of the hot, tropical colours of these impatiens makes a vibrant picture.

144

In moist, well-drained soil, *Streptocarpus* hybrids are striking accent plants.

whites, can provide the finishing touch to the subtropical garden. All large-flowering hybrids come from *S. rexii*, the Cape primrose.

Hibiscus trionum is the lowest-growing of the hibiscuses—up to 60 cm (24 in.). Native to New Zealand, its petals are a soft lemon and the centres a dramatic dark purple with gold stamens—a captivating combination. *H. trionum* tends to be biennial but, once established, keeps reappearing. It needs an open site and, when grown in light, dry soils, which it tolerates happily, tends to be prostrate; when grown in richer soils it is more upright. The other New Zealand species, *H. diversifolius*, is a shrub reaching 2 m (6.5 ft) in height. Its flowers are similar but have less appeal as they do not open.

Not every warm-climate gardener has moist conditions, and those whose plots produce better aloes than aroids should consider growing species that prefer dry conditions. But even moist gardens have their drier spots. So, for both warm-dry climate gardens and those with a lack of moisture in certain areas, here are some accent plants that like dry conditions.

From gardens to the cut-flower market, *Anigozanthos*, the kangaroo paw, from western Australia, has been an unrivalled success story. *A. flavidus*, the yellow kangaroo paw, is probably the easiest to grow, but many cultivars, particularly the dwarf 'Bush Gems' series, have been bred to include lime-green, deep red, and bright shades of pink. They prefer sandy soil, disliking cold and high humidity—and can be ravaged by snails.

Closer to the ground, *Clianthus formosus* deserves a place in a warm-climate garden but certainly not in a humid environment, for it is a trailing desert plant. If you live in the land of aloes, this ground-cover is for you. The claw-shaped flowers, a few centimetres from ground level, are a sizzling red and black. Its common name is Sturt's desert pea, and it's an annual that reproduces readily.

Lotus berthelottii is scarlet flowered and low growing. In the right spot—hot, dry, bordering on arid—it can be a marvellous little trailing plant, with eye-catching pointed flowers held erect, and feathery, bluish foliage.

Anigozanthos manglesii is drought-tolerant and easy to grow. Its unusual and colourful flowers make it an ideal accent for drier parts of the garden.

145

The Poor Knights lily, *Xeronema callistemon*, is a spectacular sight in flower.

Romneya coulteri is another plant for warm, dry deserts. It's a native of California—a scented poppy with large, crepey, white petals with intense gold centres—and it should certainly find a place in the subtropical garden. Don't attempt to grow it unless the site is dry, even parched, and sunny, with perfect drainage. In the right conditions they'll take off in a sprawling (2 x 2.5 m/6.5 x 8 ft) tangle, which needs a radical chop in late autumn. *R. trichocalyx* is said to be a superior version of *R. coulteri*.

The flowers of *Xeronema callistemon*, the Poor Knights lily, are spectacular. They're a brilliant scarlet, held on arching stems, sometimes almost horizontally, like giant toothbrushes. The flowering is a sight worth waiting for—and the wait could be up to five years. A compact, clumping plant, with shiny, sword-like leaves up to 75 cm (30 in.) long, *X. callistemon* does best in conditions most like the high sea-swept cliffs it comes from: rocky, gravelly, fast-draining, almost soil-less. And because it has adapted to finding footholds in cracks and fissures on these cliff faces, it is very much at home in a root-bound pot.

Beschorneria yuccoides is another clump-forming plant with grey-green leaves up to 1 m (3 ft) long. In spring it produces thick, coral-red flower-stalks bearing bright green flowers enclosed in rosy pink bracts. The flower-spike is very striking and has the advantage of remaining attractive, either on the plant or indoors, for up to six weeks.

Then there are succulents and cacti, which offer striking shapes as well as flower colour. For bright flowering plants, consider some of the lower-growing aloes, such as *Aloe barbadensis* (syn. *A. vera*), or the succulent *Kalanchoe blossfeldiana*, with flowering hybrids in yellow, orange, pink, red and purple. *K. blossfeldiana* can flower intermittently all year round, and, when not in flower, their fleshy, bright green leaves are neat and attractive (to 25 cm/10 in.). Plants will flower better in full sun; they can take some drought but must have perfect drainage. Kalanchoes are very easy in pots, baskets and raised rock gardens.

Aeonium arboreum is a 1 m (3 ft) high succulent with sculptured rosettes of spathulate leaves. It's a striking plant and easy to grow in light soil, preferring half-shade. Even more striking, at least in providing dramatic contrast, is the purple cultivar 'Schwarzkopf'. Both plants are short-lived and produce golden flowers on two- to three-year-old stems.

Echeveria pulvinata, the plush plant, has velvety green leaves, red-edged in autumn, in full rosettes to 30 cm (12 in.) high and 50 cm (20 in.) or more wide. It bears red flowers in spring. Another succulent, *Dudleya pulverulenta* has large, strap-like rosettes in silvery grey, and it too produces red flowers in spring and summer, growing to about 60 cm (24 in.). *Borzicactus aurantiacus* is a small (10 x 40 cm/2.5 x 10 in.) cactus, which grows in intriguing spheres, from which orange-yellow flower-spikes extend in summer.

One of the most fascinating leaf structures in all the plant world is that of the spiral aloe, *Aloe polyphylla*. Forming a perfect ascending spiral from the outer edges to the centre, *A. polyphylla* captivates attention wherever it's grown.

Finally, the orchid cactus, *Epiphyllum*, is a cinch to grow and has rich, magnificent flowers. These succulent, all-tolerant pot and basket plants, found indoors and out, are a must in the exotic garden. Their flowers, and in some cases their scents, are vibrant and dazzling. Epiphyllums need semi-shade, water and humidity in summer, but are otherwise easy to grow.

Aeonium arboreum 'Schwarzkopf' (left) and *Aloe polyphylla* are two succulents that can provide interest in dry areas of the subtropical garden.

147

Bromeliads

Bromeliads are to the exotic garden what perennials are to the traditional one: they're the lower-growing accents and finishing touches. But whereas perennials are bound by limitations of site and soil, bromeliads, which don't need soil to thrive, can grow as easily perched on a pergola as in the ground. Bromeliads are designer plants.

A slim paperback volume by Victoria Padilla entitled *Bromeliads*—recommended reading for the newcomer—has the subtitle 'beautiful, impressive and easy to grow'. This captures their attributes exactly. Beautiful: species and cultivars together cover every conceivable colour, often blending three or even four colours into inspired combinations, with patterns ranging from stripes and spots to dapplings and bandings. Impressive: from startling to spectacular, in shape and form they're bold and distinctive, and their symmetry intrigues. Easy to grow: their ease of culture is their trump card. There is, however, a misconception that they're tricky. They're not. Perhaps this mistaken view is held by people who regard bromeliads as rainforest creatures, needing conditions as close as possible to their forest habitat. While some bromeliads do, in fact, carpet the floor of Amazonian jungles, many grow naturally in quite unforest-like places, including deserts. Moreover, they've proved remarkably adaptable to all the alien and artificial places that humans have contrived to put them. As Victoria Pandilla has observed, there is probably no group of plants that have proved more amenable to living in enclosed human habitats than the *Bromeliaceae*. The important point for the subtropical gardener, though, is that all bromeliads, with perhaps the exception of the genus *Cryptanthus*, thrive outside.

Although some species are terrestrial, the majority of bromeliads, and certainly those most widely available, are epiphytes whose natural habitat is on trees, stumps or rocks, to which they attach themselves. They use their roots for anchorage, not feeding (although there has been some debate among botanists about whether some trace nutrients come through the roots), deriving their nourishment from the air ('air plants') or through their central water reservoir or urn. Bromeliads are not parasites. Anyone who has seen the bromeliad Spanish moss (*Tillandsia usneoides*) festooning trees in the southern states of the United States may be forgiven for thinking it a parasite, for the 'moss' has no apparent means of feeding. Like many others of its genus, it comes from high peaks in the Andes, from coastal escarpments and rainless deserts, and its minimal nutritional requirements are met through absorption from the air around it.

Bromeliads with built-in reservoirs, called urns or vases, take their sustenance more conspicuously. Keep watch on a summer's evening and you'll see mosquitoes laying eggs in that bromeliad you watered an hour ago. Watch the lavae hatch into little wrigglers within the plant's urn, and before long there will be a small spider's web over the entrance to catch emerging new mosquitoes. And if there should be a drought, watch the soup dry up to a sticky mess. In the wild, of course, the process is greatly extended to include tree frogs, small reptiles, invertebrates, and even species of aquatic carnivorous bladderworts that have adapted to the urn life of bromeliads. From the wastes and decomposing matter of all these living things, the bromeliads derive nutrients.

In the home garden, the urns naturally collect all available moisture, including dew, but will need filling in dry weather. Some species can manage without for longer than others. Occasional foliar feeding with liquid fish or marine-based sprays is of benefit, but be wary of chemicals; organic derivatives are safest. In particular, avoid any use of spray adhesion agents such as oil, as bromeliads breathe through their leaves and such applications are fatal.

Bromeliads can be grown on almost any surface and in almost any medium, provided there is air circulation and water can drain away from their roots. However, chemically treated timber and galvanised or copper-

Opposite: *Aechmea fasciata* in flower—powder pink with lilac stamens.

Opposite, below: *Vriesea fosteriana* 'Rubra' displays deep colours with a high lustre.

A rich display of mixed bromeliads: a single *Neoregelia concentrica* is in the centre foreground; immediately behind is a *Guzmania* 'Cherry' surrounded by other mixed species, including the tall, upright *Billbergia*, while at the back, a tree fern stump supports a large number of plants of *Neoregelia* 'Fireball'.

Bromeliads combine effectively with ferns. Colourful *Neoregelia* hybrids (red centres) are grouped above a *Nidularium fulgens*.

treated metal should be avoided, since these leach out their chemicals. Pots obviously make suitable growing places, and scoria makes a good root-anchoring medium, though bark, peat, charcoal and perlite are often used. Stumps and logs can also provide sites for bromeliads. The rougher the surface, the easier it is for the bromeliad to gain a footing. Start them off by tying them on with natural fibre twine or something soft. Driftwood can be positioned imaginatively, the holes and crevices being used for anchorage. Bromeliads can also be attached to trees. Tying is not the only means of attaching bromeliads. Glues such as paper adhesive or PVA are often used, and for the delicate, spidery tillandsias that like dry places and are best indoors, a couple of dressmakers' pins are all you need.

Like palms, bromeliads are best in groups; solitary specimens are less successful in the landscape. If there isn't a suitable tree, try making your own. Any branches or timber will do, but a tall tree fern log is by far the most successful—the dark fibrous surface shows their colours to best advantage. To maintain a natural appearance, make use of materials like sphagnum moss or coconut fibre to retain moisture around the plant while it is becoming established. Perhaps the easiest, and certainly one of the most dramatic, ways of displaying bromeliads in the garden is to let the plants grow on a mound of rocks.

Compared with rockeries and tree trunks, pots may seem unadventurous places for bromeliads, but don't underrate the portability of pots. They have the advantage when it comes to arranging and regrouping, filling gaps or

Neoregelia concentrica, with eye-catching urns.

The merging olive-green and claret shades of these *Neoregelia* hybrids are typical of the colours found in this genus.

enlivening drab corners. Don't forget, too, that bromeliads reproduce through side-shooting offspring—sometimes called pups—and, when these are severed from the parent plant, they're best put in pots to develop.

The genera in the *Bromeliaceae* family include some 2000 species and thousands of hybrids. Different genera tend to be found growing at different levels in the wild: *Tillandsia* species are among the highest and driest, the lichen-like Spanish moss belonging in this group; *Neoregelia* species grow on trees and rocks and in South America's rainforest, where there is bright light, half-day to full sun and reasonable moisture; *Aechmea* species come a little lower down, preferring, on the whole, more shade than neoregelias; while on the forest floor are the sheltered, shaded and protected *Vriesea*, *Guzmania* and *Nidularium* genera.

These are just some of the better-known and widely grown genera. There are, of course, many others, but such is the work of breeders and hybridists that the range of size and form, pattern and colour within these few genera

Left: Mixed with other foliage plants, a *Vriesea hieroglyphica* is surrounded by *Neoregelia* hybrids.

Right: Epiphytic bromeliads grow well on logs and tree stumps, and can be used this way in imaginative landscaping. These *Aechmea pineliana* species are growing on a tree fern stump over water.

alone offers choices by the hundreds for the home gardener. Take the easily grown and highly successful species *Neoregelia carolinae* (syn. *N. meyendorfii*). These wide-leaved, medium-sized rosette plants produce brilliant central colourings, which glow for months on end. Within the range of colours (orange, tangerine, crimson, magenta, lilac-purple) there are also variegations (cream edging, cream centres, cream blotches), as well as differences in leaf point (sharp or rounded) and in flower. *N. carolinae* is recommended as a beginner's plant because it is undemanding, apart from its need for light shade and moderate moisture. Other neoregelias with eye-catching colour that are equally easy to grow include: *N. carolinae* var. *tricolor* (white-striped leaves that become pink with age), *N. spectabilis* (olive-green with red tips, known as the painted fingernail plant), *N.* 'Painted Desert' (red-tipped green leaves blotched with red), *N. fosteriana* (dark burgundy) and *N. concentrica* (lilac centre).

An even easier beginner's plant, though not to everyone's liking because of its spines, is *Dyckia*, a star-shaped, terrestrial succulent that can take any drained soil in sun or shade, hot or cold—even frosts—and requires regular moisture. *Hechtia* species are similarly rugged, spined and succulent-like, and need little care. Many *Billbergia* species are, like dyckias, spring flowering and almost as tolerant, though not of sun; *B. nutans* has hanging, beautifully constructed flowers in lime-green with purple-blue edges and pink bracts, which make them deservedly popular.

Billbergia nutans is as small and slim as *Vriesea imperialis* is large and lavish. Vrieseas are among the larger garden-grown bromeliads, producing stiff, shiny leaves often speckled or with cross banding, from which grow the flattened inflorescences like swords. Vrieseas are useful for highlighting moist and shady spots in the garden, where their wide leaves and upright growth habit can attract attention. In general, most medium-sized vrieseas are epiphytes, while the larger species grow terrestrially. The imposing grand duke *V. imperialis* can reach 1 m (3 ft) or more in height, 1.5 m (5 ft) wide, with a flower-spike over 2 m (6.5 ft) tall. *V. hieroglyphica* is similarly striking. As the name implies, the leaves are densely decorated with markings reminiscent of hieroglyphics. *V. fenestralis* has a network of green and yellow markings on the leaves, and its cultivar 'Snow King' is sprinkled with white. Smaller species include *V. ensiformis* (light green leaves with a trace of mauve, red bracts with yellow petals), *V. platynema* (bluish green leaves, red bracts with yellow petals) and *V. splendens* (green leaves with dark purplish bands).

Among the shade-loving guzmanias and nidulariums, recommended species and cultivars include *Guzmania sanguinea* (rosette of green leaves tinted red), *G. lingulata* (green with brilliant red bracts, and *G.* 'Orangeade' (yellow-green plant with orange inflorescence); *Nidularium billbergioides* (dark green with orange bract), *N. innocentii* (wide, dark green leaves and deep red inner rosette), *N. innocentii* var. *striatum* (white-striped leaves) and *N. regelioides* (shiny, mottled green with rosy inner rosette).

Ananas is a genus of only eight species, all terrestrials, with spiny margins and purple-blue flower petals, but with the exception of *A. comosus*, the pineapple, this genus is not widely grown. Ananas are mostly too large and too prickly to grow as ornamentals, although there is a dwarf species from the cool and arid Andes, *A. nanus*, which could prove to be an interesting pot plant.

You will learn which plant grows best in which spot from either your own experience or the experience of others. You'll soon find out if the sun is too strong (leaf burn), if the light isn't strong enough (poor leaves), if the air's too cold ('crown chilling' in the central vase), if the air's too dry (shrivelling leaves) or if the wind's too strong (damaged leaves). Retail or mail-order nurseries usually give good advice, as do bromeliad societies—there's a society in almost every city in the world—or, failing these, read books on the subject (see page 169).

Although many bromeliads are undemanding and some, like dyckias, just about neglect-proof, it's also true that better performance follows better care. So if you want them to look their best, feed them with foliar sprays—especially the 'air plants'—clean them with mist sprays and wipe them with a cloth if necessary, and groom them if they shed old leaves. Lack of air movement can sometimes cause crown rot in the vase of some species, especially if temperatures drop, but this can usually be cured with fungicides such as Benlate. As for pests and diseases, bromeliads have it all over those other plants whose tender stems get sucked and chewed. Occasionally new growth or flower-spikes get attacked, but on the whole bromeliads are resistant.

When garden perennials put on their colour, their display may last for days or weeks. When bromeliads light up, they glow for six months or more. And the colours are lustrous, vibrant and startling. They're exotic plants—and they belong in exotic gardens.

Nidularium fulgens grows well among rocks in a shady location, its bright scarlet centre contrasting dramatically with the light green leaves.

153

Ferns

Ferns create a special magic: wherever they grow they cast a feeling of cooling, soothing freshness. They make splendid ground-concealing fillers under taller species or in shady spots where humidity is high, but they are not suitable for dry climates. Where the climate lacks moisture, it would be better to choose some of the easy-going bromeliads (such as dyckias) or drought-tolerant succulents. While one or two fern species can, in fact, put up with a bit of dryness, most crave moisture.

Ferns evolved their survival mechanism back in primordial times when the earth was shrouded with cloud, so, unlike plants that evolved later, they are able to photosynthesise in low light conditions. Shade is vital for most ferns. Even those tree ferns that are known to be sun-tolerant—*Cyathea smithii*, for example—can only take sunlight after their crowns have matured for ten to twelve years. As well as shade, they must have moisture. This means moist air, moist soil, moist roots—but freely circulating moisture that allows for aeration. Stagnant, waterlogged ground will kill ferns. A close inspection of any seemingly saturated fern gully or soakage area in the wild will show that water movement is, in fact, constant, and the ground water is always fresh and never sour. If your garden lacks sufficient natural moisture, then regular watering with a hose is best done using the finest possible misting attachment. For coastal gardeners, the news is good, for although ferns need gentle air movement rather than strong winds—and certainly not howling gales—healthy, well-cared-for plants can prove surprisingly tolerant of coastal air and salt-laden breezes, if not excessive.

As for soil, ferns are not very fussy about pH levels, provided there is organic content and decomposing matter, although the majority of species prefer slightly acid soils with occasional additions of dolomite. Blood and bone is beneficial. A constant supply of decomposing leaves from deciduous trees meets all their requirements, and serious fern-growers should consider making their own leaf mould in piles or boxes by collecting it six months in advance and allowing it to pack down under its own weight until well rotted.

If ferns become an important part of the garden—initial captivation leads easily to total obsession!—then it would be best to read more fully on the subject. The list of species that follows is but a sampling of the large number—several hundred—that can be grown in a subtropical garden. These ferns have been chosen for their good appearance, cultivation reliability and availability.

Prominent among the assortment of ferns bordering this shaded path are two specimens of *Blechnum discolor*; on the left of the photograph is *Polypodium diversifolium*; the tree fern on the right is *Cyathea australis*.

Adiantum raddianum (formerly *A. cuneatum*), the maidenhair fern, has been around a long time and makes a delightful ground-cover when well sheltered. But, more importantly, *A. raddianum* has given rise to a host of tempting cultivars, including the exquisite 'Pacific Princess' (syn. 'Pacific Maid') and the very delicate 'Gracillimum' (a mound of green fairy floss). All maidenhair ferns grow well in pots, need care—especially protection from insects and slugs—in the ground, and grow to around 30–50 cm (12–20 in.) in height.

Aspleniums, or spleenworts, grow both terrestrially and epiphytically, and almost all come from rainforests. *Asplenium oblongifolium* (formerly *A. lucidum*) is one of the larger species and well known in northern New Zealand. It develops a slowly spreading clump, reaches around 1 m (3 ft) in height, and grows easily in containers or in the ground in filtered sun. *A. shuttleworthianum*, from the Pacific Islands, is smaller (to 40 cm/16 in.) and daintier of frond. *A. aethiopicum*, or shredded spleenwort, is slightly tougher than other species, can be grown on rocks, and is especially useful in the garden because it's never attacked by slugs and snails. It grows to around 45 cm (18 in.). *A. bulbiferum* is the popular indoor fern known as the hen and chicken fern because it is so easily propagated from plantlets. It grows to over 1 m (3 ft) and is very adaptable in the garden. *A. flaccidum* is renowned for its very weeping form and its surprisingly leathery, thin fronds. Its growth habit is very variable, but it makes a good pot or basket fern. *A. terrestrie* and *A. lividum* are also worth seeking out. Most aspleniums benefit from an occasional light dressing of lime.

The light green, feathery fronds of *Asplenium bulbiferum* look superb in any situation.

This mixed planting of ferns shows contrasting leaf forms and textures: *Pteris cretica* (top, left); *Asplenium haurakiensis* (top, centre); *Doodia aspera* (top, right) and *Asplenium aethiopicum* (foreground).

Pteris cretica is a striking and very distinctive 'brake' (the common name for all pteris ferns), with long, pencil-thin fingers hanging into an elegant mound 40–60 cm (16–24 in.) high. Reliably easy to grow, *P. cretica* is good in pots and in the ground, where it gives strong textural interest. It responds well to liquid fertilising during warm months. Of a dozen or more cultivars, *P. cretica* 'Albo-lineata' (sometimes sold as a separate species) is worth obtaining for its white stripes running the length of each segment. *P. argyraea*, a naturally variegated species, is popular worldwide as an indoor plant. Outside it needs sheltered warmth. Its fronds have a fuller, more feathery form than the thin fingers of *P. cretica*.

Polypodium polypodioides is low growing (10–30 cm/4–12 in.) and makes an excellent basket fern. Although cold-sensitive, it is noted for its tolerance of dryness. (The fronds are curled, which reduces evaporation.) There are other polypodiums, differing in frond shape but sharing the tough, very scaly texture of *P. polypodioides*. Most grow to around 20–50 cm (8–20 in.).

Osmunda regalis, or royal fern, contrasts both in size and moisture needs. It can reach a height of over 2 m (6.5 ft) and likes wet soils. It's a splendidly fresh and exuberant fern and, because it grows well on water margins, can be used imaginatively and usefully in water landscaping.

Todea barbara is similarly large and handsome. Growing up to 1.5 m (5 ft) tall, at maturity it can produce robust, dense, multiple crowns bearing bright green fronds. *T. barbara* is recommended for home gardens because it adapts to most soils and conditions.

Mixed ferns including *Blechnum capense* (left) and *Nephrolepis cordifolia* (right) grow well in deep shade, contrasting with impatiens.

Davallias—often called rabbit's foot or hare's foot ferns because of their above-ground, wandering, furry rhizomes—are mostly epiphytic by nature and so can tolerate some dryness. Their fronds are fresh and airy, feathery and soft to touch. *Davallia plumosa* is more leathery than most, and its colouring is a lot darker. It grows to 40 cm (16 in.) and likes humidity, warmth and air movement. *D. fejeensis* grows larger, up to 1 m (3 ft) in height, is very long-lived—individual fronds may last for two years—and has particularly fine, feathery fronds. *D. tasmanii*, native only to the Three Kings Islands off the coast of New Zealand, is hardy, cold-resistant and not for really hot spots, but has the unusual virtue of thriving close to the sea.

Nephrolepis species are the common fishbone ferns, Boston ferns and ladder ferns. More than any others, they seem to adapt to widely varying conditions. There are even collectors or purists who reject nephrolepis as too easy to grow, as weeds in fact. But this means that for low-maintenance gardens they're a boon. When well grown in moist conditions, *Nephrolepis cordifolia* (to 80 cm/32 in.) can contribute much to the exotic garden. A smaller New Zealand native species, *Nephrolepis* sp., is daintier and not as rampant, and is without the tubers characteristic of *N. cordifolia*.

Pityrogramma chrysophylla, native to the West Indies, has naturalised itself in Samoa but is a worthwhile garden fern in the subtropics. It grows to about 50 cm (20 in.), and its delicate fronds have a waxy powder on the undersides. This can be gold but also white, grey or pale yellow. It grows well in any drained soil, tolerates sun, and makes a good container plant. *P. triangularis*, the gold-backed fern, is more readily available and is common in North America. It forms a rosette of dark green, triangular fronds, with a dusting of gold powder on the undersides. It tolerates sun, which makes the gold more pronounced, and is easily grown but benefits from care.

Christella dentata is also one of those neglect-proof plants that pop up everywhere, grow easily, but look much the better for a bit of care. *C. dentata* is fresh and graceful, forms a dense rosette (when well grown), reaches a height of 80 cm (32 in.), and can take any soil from acid to alkaline, along with shade or full sun. It looks best, though, when given plenty of water.

Lastreopsis, native to Australia and Norfolk Island, is almost as easy to grow. It forms pleasing clumps of dense, lacy fronds—bluish green in some species—which reach 80 cm (32 in.). This fern should be grown more often. *L. velutina* is a slow-growing New Zealand native; *L. marginans*, from Australia, has very dark fronds. All need plenty of shade.

Blechnums are classics among ferns. A large genus, *Blechnum* includes some of the lushest and shiniest-fronded ferns in a wide variety of shapes and forms. *Blechnum brasiliense* is sometimes called the Brazilian tree fern but should not be, for two reasons: it doesn't grow a true trunk, and the name is easily confused with the Brazilian fern tree, *Schizolobium parahybum*, a towering tree (see page 51). Its strong fronds, stiffly arching from the central crown, make it a very handsome fern. It grows to 1.5 m (5 ft) and prefers acid, loamy soil in shade. *B. capense* grows even larger (2.8 m/8.5 ft) and thrives in moisture.

Cheilanthes are grown less frequently but are worth seeking out. On the whole they can tolerate somewhat drier conditions, and *Cheilanthes brownii*

is exceptional in that it comes from quite arid and sunny areas of Australia. Another survivor of sun, but a low-growing, creeping fern and one needing more moisture, is the New Zealand native epiphyte *Pyrrosia serpens*. It's an agreeably tough fern that can be encouraged to climb on trees.

A good-looking fern from Hawaii, *Sadleria cyatheoides* makes a decorative garden subject because its neat crown of arching fronds (to over 1 m/3 ft tall) makes it seem like a miniature tree fern. It does well in organically enriched soil in shade and is recommended.

Didymochlaena truncatula is a glossy, dark-leaved fern, widely distributed around the globe and prized as much for its lustre as for its symmetry. New leaves are often tinged with pink or red. And because it's a shade-lover intolerant of any sun, it does well indoors. This is a choice fern that grows to a little over 1 m (3 ft) high.

Ferns are most effective planted in close communities, as they grow in the wild. A large *Blechnum capense* is prominent in this group (right), underneath a young *Dicksonia squarrosa*. In the centre is *Polystichum brauni*, and the small, dark green species to the left is *Peltaea falcatum*.

Another species of fresh appearance that insists upon shaded conditions is *Arachniodes aristata* (around 1 m/3 ft). It, too, has fronds that are dark and shiny, but they're a lot more prickly than most. Arachniodes is fairly easy to grow and, once established, can tolerate short dry spells.

Polystichums are like blechnums and polypodiums in that these genera account for the majority of fern species, especially those most common in cultivation. There are many, many polystichums; some, like *Polystichum acrostichoides*, are tolerant of cold and frost, but most originated in warm climates. All adapt better to outdoor conditions than indoors, and most prefer slightly acid soils.

For all of these species, the dimensions given have been confined to height. It goes without saying that all ferns spread. Some, like the tree-climbing twiner *Pyrrosia serpens*, are snake-like (as the name implies) in growth habit, but most spread out as they reach up. Width is easily allowed for—and any that outspread acceptable distances are not harmed by grooming.

One species, though, that outspreads all others (excluding tree ferns) is *Marattia salicina*. In frond length alone it excels. Native to Australia and New Zealand, the king fern deserves its name: it can reach 3.5 m (11.5 ft) or more in height, while individual fronds can measure 3 m (10 ft) in length and more than 1 m (3 ft) in width. So grow it if you have the space. *M. salicina* likes moist, rich soil, shelter from wind and sun, high humidity, and supplementary watering in summer.

Orchids

Orchids are said to be connoisseurs' plants. They are, but they're also for everybody. Though often thought of as exotic and rare, orchids are not strange, demanding or difficult—in fact, some of them are remarkably easy to grow. At the same time, their flowers are so exceptionally elegant that in the subtropical garden, to which many species are perfectly suited, they seem like luxurious extras. And they're particularly worthwhile for gardeners with small spaces or balcony gardens.

The *Orchidaceae* family is astonishingly large, with perhaps 700 or 800 genera and 20–30,000 species. Of that vast number, most people are familiar with only a handful and most orchid specialists with a few more than that. Some are terrestrial and some epiphytic. With orchids it is essential that the conditions of the plants' native habitat be reproduced in the home garden. This requirement has been simplified by the wide availability of special potting mixes and fertilisers.

The bright colours of the easily grown crucifix orchid, *Epidendrum radicans*, stand out against a background of foliage.

Cymbidiums grow as epiphytes in the wild. They can also be grown this way in cultivation, although it is more usual to see them planted in containers.

All of the following orchids will grow outdoors in mild, frost-free climates and do well in pots, on trees, under shade, on tree fern posts, in hanging baskets or in the ground.

Epidendrum radicans, the crucifix orchid, is an epiphyte with tall, cane-like stems that develop aerial roots. Newer hybrids of this species have been produced in a range of colours including red, pink, orange, mauve and white. As long as they have drainage, these orchids will grow anywhere—in pots, on logs, in the ground, in sun or shade.

Coelogyne cristata comes from high altitudes in Northern India and so likes fairly cool conditions. The flowers are opulent—gleaming white petals with golden striped centres hanging in rich displays. It grows easily in constricting containers and blooms in winter and spring.

Dendrobiums are native to the Pacific and Asia, but the Australian native species *Dendrobium falcorostrum* is the one most easily grown in subtropical gardens. An epiphyte, it is ideal for growing on trees and reaches about 20 cm (8 in.) tall; its creamy white flowers with dark red lips open in spring and are richly scented. *D. speciosum*, the rock orchid, also an epiphyte, has arching stems of fragrant, yellow flowers. This species will grow in full sun.

Encyclia cochleata, another epiphytic orchid, produces upright spikes of green flowers with dark purple-brown lips—an intriguing arrangement—which can appear intermittently throughout the year. It needs semi-shade and grows to 30 cm (12 in.).

Cymbidiums are among the best-known orchids, and there are numerous species and hybrids. In the wild they grow terrestrially or as epiphytes, but in cultivation they are most commonly grown in containers. They can, however, be planted in the ground, but they must have perfect drainage and partial shade. They are ideally suited to growing in tree fern rings. The tall, arching flower-spikes can reach up to 1 m (3 ft). With so many spectacular named cultivars, it's impossible to single out any—suffice to say that they range from palest ivory through greens, yellows and pinks to deep, glowing burgundy.

Sarcochilus hartmannii is an Australian native fast growing in popularity among enthusiasts. Small (to 15 cm/6 in.), fragrant (with the common name of orange blossom orchid) and epiphytic, all *Sarcochilus* species are gems, but *S. hartmannii* is particularly recommended—its single flower-spike produces up to twenty or more blooms in glistening white with brown spots.

Lycaste species, or virgin orchids, have striking, three-petalled flowers in whites and pastels with contrasting centres. Grown epiphytically, they have to be kept fairly dry in winter but need plentiful water in summer—and no direct sun.

Paphiopedilum species are the celebrated slipper orchids, and *P. insigne* is the species most likely to be found growing in the urban garden in the subtropics. They're fairly easy to grow, preferring small pots and containers—placed in or out of the ground—with a moisture-retentive mix of sandy soil, charcoal and fine bark. They like year-round humidity and, in winter and early spring, reveal their exotic, pouch-like flowers in light green or white with dark blotches.

Oncidium orchids, with tall flower-spikes arching to over 1 m (3 ft), bear flowers in yellows and browns (a few hybrids come in pinks or whites), which have earned them the popular name of dancing dolls. They are epiphytic and require sharp drainage for their roots, which rot easily.

Zygopetalum species are deservedly popular. They're among the few orchids whose flowers are blue (well, mauve-blue) and gorgeously scented. Since they're damaged by rain, they're not the easiest to grow outside in the subtropics. They need high humidity and shade, though they're tolerant of winter sun.

These container-grown cymbidiums are flowering profusely.

163

Water and Bog Plants

One of the distinguishing features of the subtropical garden is its natural appearance—not highly formal or contrived. Some call it a wild garden. Formal pools and ornate central fountains go well with the stately gardens of northern Europe, but in the exotic garden, where clumps of swords meet hanging climbers or fronds of tree fern in unfettered exuberance, where the ground is more likely to be bark-strewn than tile-glazed, such pools may seem out of place. The pool that looks best in the exotic garden is the pool that looks best in nature.

Plants for ponds are often classified into three groups: oxygenating plants, which live on, but mostly in, the water, absorbing nutrients through their leaves rather than their roots while usefully controlling the growth of algae and improving the water quality; floating plants, anchored at the bottom with their leaves and flowers floating on the surface—the best-known of these is, of course, the waterlily; and bog or marginal plants, which grow naturally at the water's edge. Suppliers of pond equipment are the best source of oxygenating plants, together with good advice about maintaining water clarity. Fish can also be very useful, helping to aerate the water and eating any insects on plants, while cleaning up debris and minute organisms.

Flowering aquatics are the real joy of a water garden, and there are two classic beauties: the waterlily and the lotus. Waterlilies, *Nymphaea* species, are deservedly admired—and they're extremely easy to grow. All they need is good-quality soil for their roots, and water to float on. Containers set on the bottom of the pond or special wire waterlily baskets are used most often, though if the pond has a foundation of rich soil, the waterlilies can be planted directly into it.

Waterlilies are divided into hardy and tropical varieties. While hardy varieties are planted out in early spring and will bloom throughout summer, tropical waterlilies can be left over winter in their ponds, and their blooming time is later in the season. (Some cool-climate gardeners do successfully lift them and store them indoors over winter.) Hardy waterlilies come in shades of yellow, pink, white, cream and red. Tropical waterlilies have flowers in blues, mauves and violet, and the blooms are held well above the water. The long stalks enable them to be picked. With their rich, hyacinth-like fragrance, the cut flowers will last for up to two weeks in cool weather, less in warmer weather. Most waterlilies thrive best in water 30–60 cm (12–24 in.) deep, but the ideal depth for tropical varieties is 25–35 cm (10–14 in.).

This peaceful water garden is planted with hardy waterlilies and edged with blue-flowered *Pontederia cordata*, the pickerel rush, the huge, quilted leaves of *Gunnera manicata* and the elegant, arching *Bambusa gracilis*.

Cultivars that reliably produce fine quality flowers include: 'Blue Stellata' (sky-blue), 'Black Prince' (deep purple), 'Blue Beauty' (deep purple-blue), 'A. E. Seibert' (mauve-pink), 'Pink Star' (clear pink), 'Mrs George Pring' (pure white), 'Colonel Linburg' (mauve-blue), 'Rose Star' (rose-pink), 'American Beauty' (deep pinkish red), and 'Yellow Dazzler'.

Waterlilies rarely suffer from pests or diseases. Occasionally a little nymph insect gets into the stems, but fish soon clean these up. The other possible attackers are aphids, which are best dealt a blast of high-pressure hosing. If they persist, try applying a weak solution of white oil, which won't hurt the fish. Waterlilies multiply readily and are best divided in autumn.

That other flowering aristocrat is, of course, the lotus, *Nelumbo nucifera*. This is the flower of biblical lineage, the symbol of purity, the revered sacred flower of Buddhism. The huge, chalice-shaped flowers, carried above the foliage on strong stems, are rose-pink and delectably fragrant. There is also a beautiful, creamy white variety, 'Alba Grandiflora'. Its round, blue-green leaves are large and smooth, and held high above the water. The flowers are followed by very attractive seed-pods. Like waterlilies, lotuses lose their leaves in winter. The dead leaves are best gathered up and removed from the pond. Plants need full sun and grow best in a depth of water around 60 cm. Lotus plants spread rapidly, are highly disease-resistant and very easy to grow—in fact, restraining their growth could be a problem.

Monochoria cyanea grows in the same depth of water as waterlilies and produces spikes of purple-blue flowers.

Other floating water plants that might be considered are: *Aponogeton* species, with oblong leaves and fragrant, white flowers (*A. distachyos* is from South Africa and tolerates cooler temperatures than the tropical *A. crispus* from Sri Lanka); the water poppy, *Hydocleys nymphoides*, which needs full sunlight and can be planted just a few centimetres below the surface—it bears yellow, poppy-like flowers throughout summer; and the floating fern *Azolla caroliniana*, which grows easily (so easily that it may need to be controlled) in sun or shade and is useful for reducing algae.

Hybrids derived from *Canna glauca* crossed with terrestrial canna hybrids are available in red, salmon-pink, yellow and burnt orange. As well as growing in full sun in the garden, they can be planted in containers of rich potting soil and submerged 15–20 cm (6–8 in.) below the surface of the water. They are also excellent as marginal plants on the banks of ponds or streams. The leaves are glaucous, and the plants grow 1.2–1.8 m (4–6 ft) tall.

With no hard edges, the natural pond merges gradually with the land, creating a marginal or bog area. This is the place to plant any of a host of wonderful species that like wet conditions. One of the most imposing marginal plants is *Gunnera manicata*, with its huge leaves like puckered umbrellas. It belongs in the (moist) subtropical garden, but will grow equally easily in cool, temperate climates. The lavish-leaved alocasias, colocasias and xanthosomas revel in damp and wet ground. Some of the new cultivars have rich colouring with darker undersides to the leaves, or long, purple-black stalks that contrast with the surrounding lighter greens. Other aroids such as aglaonemas or spathiphyllums (which grow naturally on the edges of Amazon watercourses) can be planted in the more drained areas around the

The rose-pink flowers and unusual seed-pods of the lotus, *Nelumbo nucifera*, are held above the imposing, blue-green foliage.

Edged with slabs of weathered rock, this pond set amid manicured lawns features waterlilies, irises, gunneras and a tree fern.

Grasses and small ferns planted among the rocks soften the edges of this pool filled with waterlilies. Strategically placed specimens of *Cycas revoluta* provide a strong architectural element.

pond's edge (see also pages 125–127). The hybrid *Zantedeschia* 'Green Goddess' makes a marvellous bog plant when grown in full or half-shade.

Warm-climate irises, *Iris louisiana*, prefer full sun and they, too, are superb subjects for the subtropical garden; modern hybrids are tall, profuse in flower, and come in every colour—blues and purples through reds to bright yellow.

Papyrus, *Cyperus papyrus*, is tailor-made for water margins and is easy to grow wherever there's sun, warmth and wet ground. Given conditions to its liking, it can grow as tall as 3 m (10 ft).

The sword rush, *Lepidosperma gladiatum*, is lower growing (to 1 m/3 ft) and less commonly seen than papyrus, but very easy. *Thalia geniculata* grows taller (to 2 m/6.5 ft), forming clumps with shining, oval leaves, and has violet flower-spikes. *T. dealbata*, also with violet flowers, is possibly more common and is a more cold-tolerant species widely grown in the United States. *Pontederia cordata* is another with blue flower-spikes. *Sagittaria sagittifolia*, with its arrow- shaped leaves and white flowers, is also easily grown, preferring sun and water about 25 cm (10 in.) deep.

More than any other type of garden, water gardens bring together flora and fauna in happy co-existence, with birds, fish, amphibians and plant life all adding to the gardener's enjoyment.

Recommended Reading

Adams, William Howard, *Roberto Burle Marx: The Unnatural Art of the Garden*, New York, Museum of Modern Art/Harry N. Abrams, 1991

Austin R., D. Levy and K. Veda, *Bamboo*, New York, Weatherill, 1985

Bailey, L. H. & E. Z., *Hortus Third*, London, Collier Macmillan, 1976

Bown, Deni, *Aroids: Plants of the Arum Family*, London, Century Hutchinson, 1988

Boyer, Keith, *Palms and Cycads Beyond the Tropics*, Palm and Cycad Societies of Australia, 1992

Brickell, Christopher (ed.), *The Reader's Digest Gardeners' Encyclopaedia of Plants and Flowers*, Sydney, Reader's Digest, 1991

Burras, J. K. & M. Griffiths, *Manual of Climbers and Wall Plants*, Portland, Timber Press, 1994

Cave, Yvonne, *The Succulent Garden*, Auckland, Godwit Publishing, 1996

Clay, H. F., J. C. Hubbard & R. Golt, *The Hawai'i Garden: Tropical Shrubs*, Honolulu, University of Hawaii Press, 1987

Challis, Myles, *The Exotic Garden*, London, Fourth Estate, 1988

Courtright, Gordon, *Tropicals,* Portland, Timber Press, 1988

Eliovson, S., *The Gardens of Roberto Burle Marx*, Portland, Sagapress/Timber Press, 1991

Farrelly, David, *The Book of Bamboo*, San Francisco, Sierra Club Books, 1984

Glowinski, Louis, *The Complete Book of Fruit Growing in Australia*, Melbourne, Lothian, 1991

Graf, A. B., *The Exotic Plant Manual*, New Jersey, Roehrs Company, 1978

Graf, A. B., *Tropica*, 3rd ed., New Jersey, Roehrs Company, 1986

Hobbs, Jack & Terry Hatch, *Best Bulbs for Temperate Climates*, Portland, Timber Press, 1994

Hobbs, Jack & Terry Hatch, *Bulbs for New Zealand Gardeners and Collectors*, Auckland, Godwit Publishing, 1994

Hodgson, M., R. Paine & N. Anderson, *A Guide to Orchids of the World*, Sydney, Angus & Robertson, 1991

Holttum, R. & I. Enoch, *Gardening in the Tropics*, Timber Press/Times Edition, 1991

Huntington Botanical Gardens, *Dry Climate Gardening with Succulents*, New York, Pantheon Books/Knopf Publishing Group, 1995

Jones, David, *Cycads of the World*, Sydney, Reed Books, 1993

Jones, David, *Palms in Australia*, Sydney, Reed Books, 1984

Jones, David, *Palms throughout the World*, Sydney, Reed Books, 1985

Lötschert, W. & G. Beese, *Collins Photo Guide: Tropical Plants*, Harper Collins, 1994

Macoboy, Stirling, *Exotic Perennials*, Sydney, Angus & Robertson, 1991

Macoboy, Stirling, *What Tree is That?*, Sydney, Landsowne Press, 1994

Menninger, Edwin A., *Fantastic Trees*, Portland, Timber Press, 1995

Menninger, Edwin A., *Flowering Vines of the World: An Encyclopaedia of Climbing Plants*, New York, Hearthside Press, 1970

Miller, Helen & Richard Ratcliffe, *Top Plants for Tropical Gardens*, Canberra, Australian Government Publishing Service, 1990

Morton, Julia F., *500 Plants of South Florida*, E. A. Seeman Publishing Inc., 1974

Nicholls, Christine & John, *Climbing Plants*, Auckland, Godwit Publishing, 1995

Padilla, Victoria, *Bromeliads*, New York, Crown Publishers, 1973

Pridgeon, A., *The Illustrated Encyclopaedia of Orchids*, Portland, Timber Press, 1992

Sajeva M. & Costanzo M., *Succulents: The Illustrated Dictionary*, Portland, Timber Press, 1994

Warren, William & Luca Invermizzi Tettoni, *Balinese Gardens*, London, Thames & Hudson, 1995

Warren, William & Luca Invermizzi Tettoni, *Thai Garden Style*, Singapore, Periplus, 1996

Warren, William & Luca Invermizzi Tettoni, *The Tropical Garden*, London, Thames & Hudson, 1991

Williams, Barry E. (ed.), *Growing Bromeliads*, Sydney, Kangaroo Press, 1988

List of Suppliers

Unless described as difficult to obtain, all the plants in this book are available from retail or specialist nurseries. Some suppliers sell by mail order only. Some are open by appointment only. It is advisable to write and enquire about plant lists, mail order buying, and/or opening times.

NEW ZEALAND

Courier Climbers, PO Box 2458, Tauranga, Bay of Plenty (climbing vines)

Crumps Fern Nursery, 64 Trig Road, Whenuapai, Auckland (ferns)

Enzed Subtropico, State Highway 10, RD 3, Kerikeri, Bay of Islands (palms, cycads, dracaenas)

Etheringtons, PO Box 3046, Richmond, Nelson (African trees)

Exotic Nursery, Lamas Road, RD 1, Kaitaia, Northland (trees, ornamentals, rarities)

Flora Spectabilis, PO Box 68137, Newton, Auckland (aloes, dracaenas, succulents)

Greens Bromeliads, PDC Maungakaramea, Whangarei, Northland (bromeliads)

Isaachson's Bamboo Nursery, 833 West Coast Road, Oratia, Auckland (bamboo specialists)

Koanga Nursery, RD 1, Maungaturoto, Northland (fruit and edibles)

Landsendt, 108 Parker Drive, Oratia, Auckland (fruit specialist, palms and cycads)

Opanuku Subtropical Nursery, PO Box 21733, Henderson, West Auckland (palms, aroids and ornamentals)

Plants Galore, 11b Armstrong Place, New Lynn, Auckland (bromeliads)

Plateau Nursery, Taha Road, Waimauku, Auckland (palms)

Pukeawa Gardens, Mahoetahi Road, RD 42, Waitara, Taranaki (palms and cycads)

Russell Fransham's Subtropicals, Matapouri Bay, RD 3, Whangarei, Northland (palms, fruit and ornamentals)

Tamahunga Tropical Gardens, 140 Govan Wilton Road, Matakana, North Auckland (trees and ornamentals, rarities)

The Palm Farm, 119 Walmsley Road, Mangere, Auckland (palms and cycads)

Tropic of Auckland, ph. 445-0594 (specimen palms, cycads and shrubs)

Wharepuke Nursery and Gardens, 190 Kerikeri Road, Kerikeri, Bay of Islands (ornamentals)

AUSTRALIA

Boyds Bay Garden Centre, Cnr Pacific Highway and Boyds St, Tweed Heads NSW 2485

Carseldine Garden World, Cnr Gympie and Beams Rds, Carseldine QLD 4034

Ross Evans Home and Garden Centre, 300 Oxley Dr, Runaway Bay QLD 4216

Fairhill Native Plants, Fairhill Rd, Yandina QLD 4561

Gardenway Nurseries, 269 Monier Rd, Darra QLD 4076

Greenworld Garden Centre, 22 Gowan Rd, Sunnybank Hills QLD 4109

Hampton Gardens, 2274 Moggill Rd, Kenmore QLD 4069

Hawkins Nursery and Garden Centre, 1666 Old Cleveland Rd, Chandler QLD 4155

Melson Rock Nursery, 6 Burnett St, White Rock QLD 4868

Redwoods Garden Centre, 102 David Low Way, Sunshine Beach QLD 4567

Terania Rainforest Nursery, Bruxner Highway, Wollongbar NSW 2477

The Vireya Place, 7 Lawrence Place, Maleny QLD 4552

UNITED STATES

Bamboo Sourcery, 666 Wagnon Road, Sebastopol, CA 95472

Banana Tree, 715 Northampton St., Easton, PA 18042

Bovees Nursery, 1737 S.W. Coronado, Portland, OR, 97219

Brudy's Exotics, P.O. Box 820874, Houston, TX 77282-0874

Burt & Associates Bamboo, P.O. Box 719, Westford, MA 01886

Caladium World, P.O. Drawer 629, Sebring, FL, 33871

Carter & Holmes, No 1 Old Mendenhall Road, P.O. Box 668, Newberry SC 29108

Carter Seeds, 475 Mar Vista Dr, Vista, CA 92083

Exotica Rare Fruit Nursery, 2508-B East Vista Way, Vista, CA 92084

Floribunda Palms & Exotics, P.O. Box 635, Mt. View, HI 96771

Foliage Gardens, 2003- 128th Ave, S.E., Bellevue, WA 98005

Forest Farm, 990 Tetherow Rd., Williams, OR 97544-9599

Four Winds, P.O. Box 3538, 42186 Palm Ave., Fremont CA 94539

Garden of Delights, 14560 S.W. 14th St., Davie, FL 33325-4217

Glasshouse Works, P.O. Box 97, Church St., Stewart, OH 45778-0097

Logee's Greenhouse, 141 North St., Danielson, CT 06239

Neon Palm Nursery, 3525 Stony Point Road, Santa Rosa, CA 95407

Pineapple Place, 3961 Markham Woods Road, Longwood, FL 32779

The Plumeria People, P.O. Box 820014, Houston, TX 77282-0014

Rainbow Tropicals, Inc., P.O. Box 4038, Hilo, HI, 96720

Southern Exposure, 35 Minor St. (at Rusk), Beaumont, TX 77702

TyTy Plantation, P.O. Box 130 H. Tyty, Georgia 31793

Index

Page references in italic type indicate illustrations.

Microclimate, 12
Mina lobata, 99
Mitraria coccinea, 108
Monochoria cyanea, 167
Monstera deliciosa, 121
Montanoa bipinnatifida, 112
   hibiscifolia, 112
Moreton Bay chestnut, see *Castanospermum
   australe*
Mother-in-law's tongue, see *Sansevieria
   trifasciata*
Murraya paniculata, 109
Musa acuminata, 43
   basjoo, 45
   coccinea, 45
   mannii, 45
   ornata, 45
   x *paradisiaca*, *24*, 43
   sumatrana, 45
   velutina, *43*, 45
Myrciaria cauliflora, 24

Naranjilla, see *Solanum quitoense*
Natal plum, see *Carissa grandiflora*
Nelumbo nucifera, 167, *167*
Neodypsis decaryi, 37
Neoregelia, *149, 150*, 151, *151*
   carolinae, 152
   concentrica, *149, 151*, 152
   fosteriana, 152
   meyendorfii, see *N. carolinae*
   spectabilis, 152
Nephrolepis cordifolia, 158, *158*
Nerium oleander, 103
Nidularium, 151
   billbergioides, 153
   fulgens, *150*
   innocentii, 153
   regelioides, 153
Nikau, see *Rhopalostylis sapida*
Nymphaea, 164

Ochna serrulata, 104, *104*
Odontonema strictum, 112
Oleander, see *Nerium oleander*
Oncidium, 163
Orchid, crucifix, see *Epidendrum radicans*
   orange blossom, see *Sarcochilus hartmannii*
   rock, see *Dendrobium speciosum*
   slipper, see *Paphiopedilum*
   virgin, see *Lycaste*
Orchid tree, see *Bauhinia*
Orchids, 161–163
Osmunda regalis, 157
Ozone layer, 14

Pachystachys lutea, 108
Palm, assai, see *Euterpe edulis*
   bamboo, see *Rhapis excelsa*
   bangalow, see *Archontophoenix
   cunninghamiana*
   California fan, see *Washingtonia robusta*
   Canary Island date, see *Phoenix canariensis*
   Chinese fan, see *Livistona chinensis*
   Chinese fishtail, see *Caryota ochlandra*
   Chinese windmill, see *Trachycarpus fortunei*
   chusan, see *Trachycarpus fortunei*
   cotton, see *Washingtonia robusta*
   dwarf date, see *Phoenix roebelinii*
   dwarf palmetto, see *Sabal minor*
   European fan, see *Chamaerops humilis*
   golden cane, see *Chrysalidocarpus lutescens*
   Guadalupe, see *Brahea edulis*
   jelly, see *Butia capitata*, *Butia yatay*
   jucara, see *Euterpe edulis*

kentia, see *Howea forsteriana*
Kermadec Island, see *Rhopalostylis baueri*
   var. *cheesemanii*
king, see *Archontophoenix alexandrae*
lady, see *Rhapis excelsa*
Madagascar, see *Neodypsis decaryi*
Mexican blue hesper, see *Brahea armata*
Norfolk Island, see *Rhopalostylis baueri* var.
   baueri
parlour, see *Chamaedorea elegans*
ponytail, see *Beaucarnea recurvata*
queen, see *Syagrus romanzoffiana*
Quito, see *Parajubaea cocoides*
reed, see *Chamaedorea seifrizii*
sago, Japanese, see *Cycas revoluta*
seaforthia, see *Archontophoenix*
travellers', see *Ravenala madagascariensis*
walking-stick, see *Linospadix monostachya*
windmill, see *Trachycarpus fortunei*
Palms, 28–42
Palmgrass, see *Setaria palmifolia*
Pandorea jasminoides, 97
   pandorana, 97
Paphiopedilum insigne, 163
Parajubaea cocoides, 40
Parapara, see *Pisonia umbellifera*
Parrot tree, see *Schotia brachypetala*
Passiflora alata, 97
   amethystina, 97
   antioquiensis, 97
   caerulea, *96*, 97
   cinnabarina, 97
   coccinea, *96*, 97
   edulis, 97
   x *exoniensis*, 97
   ligularis, 24
   mollissima, 97
Passionfruit, see *Passiflora*
   banana, see *Passiflora mollissima*, *P.
   antioquiensis*
Pawpaw, see *Carica*
Peace lily, see *Spathiphyllum wallisii*
Pellionia daveauana, 129
   repens, 129
Peltaea falcatum, *159*
Peltophorum ferrugineum, see *P. pterocarpum
   pterocarpum*, 79
Peperomia marmorata, 129
   obtusifolia 'Variegata', 129
Pepino, see *Solanum muricatum*
Persea americana, 24
Petrea volubilis, 91, *91*, 94, 102
Phaedranthus buccinatorius, *91*, 92
Phaseolus caracalla, 96
Philodendron bipinnatifidum, 124
   erubescens, 124
   melanochrysum, 124
   sagittifolium, 124
   scandens, *122*, 124
   variifolium, 124
   wendlandii, 124
Phoenix canariensis, *29*, 31, *34*, 40, *44*
   dactylifera, 31, 40
   reclinata, *29*, *31*, 40
   roebelinii, *29*, *32*, 35, *44*
   rupicola, 40
   sylvestris, 40
Phormium, 57
   cookianum, 56
   tenax, 56
Physalis peruviana, 24
Pilea cadieri, 129
   nummulariifolia, 129
Pineapple, see *Ananas comosus*
Pisonia umbellifera, 50

Pityrogramma chrysophylla, 158
   triangularis, 158
Planter rings, 18
Plumbago auriculata, 102, 104, 106
   capensis, see *P. auriculata*
Plumeria obtusa, 83
   rubra, *82*, 83
Podranea ricasoliana, 98, *99*
Pohutukawa, see *Metrosideros excelsa*
Poinsettia, see *Euphorbia pulcherrima*
Polianthes tuberosa, 143
Polypodium diversifolium, *154*
   polypodioides, 157
Polystichum acrostichoides, 160
   brauni, *159*
Pomegranate, wild, see *Burchellia bubalina*
Pontederia cordata, *164*, 168
Ponytail palm, see *Beaucarnea recurvata*
Poor Knights lily, see *Xeronema callistemon*
Popcorn bush, see *Cassia spectabilis*
Poroporo, see *Solanum laciniatum*
Port St John creeper, see *Podranea ricasoliana*
Potato tree, blue, see *Solanum rantonnettii*
   vine, see *Solanum jasminoides*
Pride of Bolivia, see *Tipuana tipu*
Pritchardia gaudichaudii, 38
Prunus capollin, 24
Pseudopanax, 46, *46*
Psidium guajava, 24
Pteris argyrea, 157
   cretica, 157, *157*
Puka, see *Meryta sinclairii*
Puya alpestris, 64, *64*
   chilensis, 64
   raimondii, 64
Pyrostegia venusta, 100
Pyrrosia serpens, 159, 160

Queen of the night, see *Cestrum nocturnum*
Queensland bottle tree, see *Brachychiton
   rupestris*
   firewheel tree, see *Stenocarpus sinuatus*
   umbrella tree, see *Schefflera actinophylla*
Quisqualis indica, 97

Rabbit's foot fern, see *Davallia*
Radermacheria sinensis, 83
Rangoon creeper, see *Quisqualis indica*
Raphidophora decursiva, 124
Rata, see *Metrosideros robusta*
Ravenala madagascariensis, 43, 45
Renealmia cernua, 136
Renga-renga lily, see *Arthropodium cirratum*
Rhapis excelsa, 35
   humilis, 35
Rhodochiton atrosanguineum, 94
Rhododendron, vireya, *11*, 14, 117–120,
   117, *118*
Rhododendron christi, 120
   christianae, 119
   commonae, 120
   jasminiflorum, 119
   javanicum, 119
   konori, 119
   laetum, 119
   leucogigas, 119
   lochae, 119
   loranthiflorum, 119
   macgregoriae, 120
   orbiculare, 119
   superbum, 120
   tuba, 120
   zoelleri, 120
Rhodoleia championii, 83
Rhopalostylis baueri var. *baueri*, *34*, 39